ADVANCED PRAISE FOR
THE ANTIFRAGILE MAN

"Howdy Y'all I'm Forrie J Smith also known as Lloyd from "Yellowstone", I got that part when I's 58 years old, unknowingly I have been living and using Dr. Genes' principles, still setting goals and dreaming about things to come. This book is great for us aged men but I also feel it could be a perfect guide book for the younger males of today and for single mothers trying to raise young men on their own. God Bless and read on"

Forrie J. Smith …aka " Lloyd"
from the hit TV series "Yellowstone"

"The Antifragile Man by Dr. Gene Tynes is truly an amazing book that all men of all ages need to read and incorporate into their own lives. It is expertly crafted and extremely well thought-out based on the life and observations of Dr. Tynes. A must read for every man!"

Jeffry S. Life, MD author of The Long Life Plan:
Living to 100 and Beyond with Strength,
Vitality, Purpose, Passion and Grit.

"In a world where chaos is the new normal, The Antifragile Man delivers a powerful wake-up call to men approaching - or already living - their second half of life. Blending raw personal experience, practical wisdom, and a no-nonsense tone, Dr. Gene Tynes redefines what it means to grow stronger through adversity. More than just a guide to aging well, this book is a battle plan for thriving mentally, physically, and emotionally. With insights drawn from wilderness guiding, decades in healthcare, and the school of hard knocks, Tynes shows readers how to embrace discomfort, reprogram limiting beliefs, and develop a mindset - and body - that doesn't just endure storms, but uses them to grow. Candid, courageous, and compelling, The Antifragile Man is a must-read for any man ready to stop surviving and start dominating the next chapter of life."

Simon Bowen, Author, International Speaker, Strategic Advisor, Founder of The Models Method© and Creator of The Genius Model©

"Now that I'm over 50, I look to men like Dr. Gene Tynes for inspiration and knowledge about how I'm gonna live through the next few decades. At 65, Gene is doing the kinds of things that most guys in their 20s couldn't hack. He tackles the subject of aging with the knowledge of a Doctor and the heart and spirit of a seasoned adventurer."

Steven Rinella, #1 New York Times bestselling author and host of The MeatEater Podcast

"I know Gene Tynes author of The Antifragile Man personally. He's no BS. Every man over 50 that still wants to look good, feel good, and do good needs to incorporate his advice into their daily life. He's not a fly by night wanna-be. He's a real dude from Montana that is living large and enjoying every day."

Dean Folkvord
1997 Montana Small Business Person of the Year
Founder Wheat Montana Farms and Bakery

"There's no finish line, so stop looking for it! The Antifragile Man will help you embrace life, providing a blueprint to set the standard for your family and community as you enter the best years of your life."

John Barklow
Retired Special Ops Instructor, U.S. Military
Teaching Special-Ops forces and rescue groups how
to survive in the world's toughest environments

"Gene Tynes is THE Anti-Fragile Man. In his new book he redefines what's possible for men over 50 in mind, body, and mission. Just as he has in his own life."

Greg Gianforte
Governor of Montana

THE ANTIFRAGILE MAN

A TACTICAL GUIDE TO STRENGTH THAT DEFIES AGE

DR. GENE TYNES

The Antifragile Man

Published by GeneTough Publishing

www.GeneTough.com

© 2025 GeneTough Publishing. All rights reserved.

GeneTough Publishing is an independent imprint dedicated to powerful, purpose-driven writing that redefines strength, Antifragility, and masculinity for the modern age.

Printed in the United States of America.

Disclaimer: This book is for educational purposes only; consult your physician before making any changes to your exercise, nutrition, or lifestyle.

ISBN: 979-8-89694-362-4 - eBook

ISBN: 979-8-89694-363-1 - Paperback

ISBN: 979-8-89694-612-0 - Hardcover

ISBN: 979-8-89694-613-7 - Audiobook

"If you stop pursuing the things you are capable of, you won't stay capable for long"

DR. GENE TYNES

WHY READ THIS BOOK?

This book has been a long time in the making — a true passion project born from decades of experience, hardship, growth, and encouragement from those closest to me. It represents not only what I've learned, but what I believe must be passed on.

The Antifragile Man was written first for the man in the second half of life — the one who knows there's more gas in the tank, more to give, and more to become. But just as importantly, it was written for the younger man — especially those who've never had a real male role model to look to. If you're that younger man, consider this your head start. Your shortcut to wisdom most men earn only after years of pain.

This is not theory. It's a tactical guide to physical strength, mental clarity, and moral integrity — principles that, when adopted and practiced, will enhance *any* man's life, at *any* age.

In a world that often downplays masculinity or distorts it entirely, we must reclaim what it means to be a good man — strong, compassionate, capable, and unshakable. For older men, that means modeling it. For younger men, it means learning it before the world teaches you the wrong thing.

My hope is that this book becomes more than words on a page — that it becomes a blueprint for becoming unbreakable in the face of life's inevitable storms.

DEDICATION

To my beautiful, amazing, strong, and loving wife of 43 years, Kelly, whose unwavering belief in me has been my greatest source of strength. It was love at first sight, a moment of divine intervention that forever changed my life. Thank you for being my soulmate and my inspiration. Thank you for encouraging me to write this book.

To my incredible daughters, Sadie and Heidi, who are just like their momma. I am so blessed to be your Dad and so proud of the women you've become.

To my Sons-in Laws, Jack and Mike. I hope you will embody these ideas to help nurture all of those around you and inspire them to be the best version of themselves. I am counting on you to carry on the tradition.

And to my Heaven sent grandkids—Theo, Tyne, Zoey, and RubyGene. I hope this book will be a source of pride and inspiration for you long after I am gone from this earth. Papa loves you. I want this to be a guide for my boys regarding how to conduct themselves with confidence and humility, and as a guide for my girls to help them identify men worthy of their love.

TABLE OF CONTENTS

Why Read This Book?.. ix

Introduction: What Kind of Man Are You?............................ 1

Part 1: Awaken the Antifragile Mindset

Embracing the Age of Wisdom 17

Redefining Retirement and Purpose 27

Navigating Modernity 37

Part 2: Mental Reprogramming for Anti-Fragility

Overcoming Limiting Beliefs: How do Antifragile
Men Think And Act?.. 53

Imposter Syndrome, Self-Sabotage, and Money Mindset...... 67

Setting Proper Expectations For The Future 83

Part 3: Building the Anti-Fragile Body

A History of Physical Fitness... 95

Nutrition Simplified.. 105

Training And Recovery Simplified..................................... 123

Part 4: Thriving in Relationships, Masculinity, and Abundance

It's Okay To Be A Man 143

Love as Strength: The Antifragile Heart............................. 157

The Law of Abundance 167

Hope For The Future 177

Conclusion: Becoming The Antifragile Man...................... 191

Acknowledgments 197

About the Author 199

WHAT KIND OF MAN ARE YOU?

If your whole world turned upside down tomorrow, how would you deal with it?

The day my doctor told me I had a rare blood disorder requiring $500,000 in annual medication just to stay alive, I faced a choice every man eventually confronts: crumble under pressure or transform it into power.

Perhaps you're in a similar situation? It doesn't have to be health related, as life presents many challenges in all kinds of unique ways for all of us to face. The job you've been grinding at for years could be gone. Your savings? Down the drain. Your health? Suddenly, it's on a timer. Your future is calling, and it's asking: *What kind of man are you really?* Most men are so caught up in the daily grind that they never consider these scenarios, even though we all saw a glimpse of it in 2020.

Some men emerged from the COVID-19 pandemic stronger than ever, while others were decimated physically, financially, mentally, or all three. So what's the difference? Something separates the men who thrive in retirement from those who barely survive a year or two. But life isn't about just surviving, it's becoming the kind of man who grows stronger from the hits. This book will help you become that kind of man.

HOW DO YOU DEAL WITH THE STORMS OF LIFE?

We're living in a world where the only certainty is uncertainty. Chaos isn't just knocking at the door; it's kicked it down and made itself at home. The unexpected has become our new normal, and it's got a lot of us feeling like we're trying to navigate a minefield blindfolded. That pit in your stomach? That's the realization that simply being resilient isn't cutting it anymore. We're not just talking about weathering the storm; we're talking about *dancing in the damn rain* and coming out stronger for it. But here's the rub: most of us weren't taught how to do this. We're stuck in old patterns, clinging to outdated ideas of what it means to be a man, and it's leaving us vulnerable in a world that demands more than just grit, stubbornness, and "grinding it out."

INTRODUCING ANTI-FRAGILITY

Enter "anti-fragility," a concept that's about to flip your world view on its head. Coined by risk analyst Nassim Nicholas Taleb, it describes systems that don't just withstand chaos, but *thrive* on it. Picture this: you're not just a rock standing firm against the waves; you're a surfer, using each wave to propel you further, higher, and faster.

My friend Brian Johnson captures this beautifully in his book "Arete." He talks about how a strong wind will blow out a candle but fuel a fire. The question is, Which one are you? Are you the candle, cowering from every gust, or are you the fire, roaring higher with each challenge?

Being Antifragile means you don't just face adversity, you feast on it. It's about turning every setback into a setup for a comeback. Imagine facing life's challenges not with fear, but with a "bring-it-on" attitude. That's the power of anti-fragility, and it separates the men from the boys in today's world.

"The Antifragile Man" isn't just another self-help book gathering dust on your shelf. It's your battle plan for conquering life's chaos. We're going to dive deep into the trenches of personal development, forging an elite physique that can handle whatever life throws at you. You'll learn how to build mental fortitude that would make a Navy SEAL proud, and master strategies for career success that turn economic uncertainty into your personal gold mine. But we're not stopping there. You'll discover:

- How to turn stress into your secret weapon for growth

- The art of adaptation: becoming a chameleon in a world of constant change

- Techniques to build unshakeable confidence, even when everything around you is crumbling

- Strategies for building relationships that withstand the test of time and tragedy

By the time you finish this book, you won't just have a toolbox for success. You'll have an entire damn *workshop*, full of all the tools you will need to navigate life and its inevitable storms. It's not *if* the storm is coming; it's *when*. You'll understand that there's no such thing as losing. There's only winning or learning. And most importantly, you'll have given yourself permission to win in every aspect of your life. None of these changes will happen overnight, but if you put in the work, you can become antifragile.

WHO AM I TO GUIDE YOU?

Now, you might be wondering, "Who the hell is this guy to tell me how to live my life?" Fair question. I'm not just some armchair philosopher spouting theories. As of the writing of this book, I am 65 years old, so I am not a spring chicken, but I bet if you met me in person, you would guess I was years younger. This book is written from my perspective at this age, but it is equally applicable to younger men.

I am a Cowboy at heart. People that meet me always assume I must own a ranch somewhere.[1] My first jobs from ages 12-17 were all on ranches. I love the whole tradition of being a true cowboy. The work ethic, the outdoors, and being a man who always kept his word. The Cowboy code of ethics guides a lot of my decisions to this day.

I'm a licensed member of the Montana Association of Guides and Outfitters. That means I've led men through some of the most unforgiving terrain Mother Nature has to offer. If I can keep folks alive and thriving in the backcountry where one wrong move means game over, you bet your ass I can guide you through the urban jungle and beyond.

But my experience goes beyond the wilderness. For the first 7 years after I received my degree in Ag.Economics from Montana State University (Go Bobcats), I worked for a great company in my hometown. It payed very well and I was working my way up the corporate ladder. However, I had this burning desire down deep inside that I was capable of so much more. We will talk later in this book about how men need a challenge to feel fulfilled. One day I came home and told my wife out of nowhere that I thought I should become a Dentist. I explained,"I am really good at working with my hands, a good problem solver, and I wanted to make a difference in people's lives". She gave me one of those looks

---

[1]   I have been an "extra" in 2 film productions. One being an "Angry Rancher" in the hit series *Yellowstone* and the other being a "Royal Canadian Mounted Police" in the movie "The Untouchables" with actors Sean Connery and Kevin Costner

(you know the look men) but she believed in me and has always supported me. It truly was one of those "here, hold my beer" moments. So I applied to Dental Schoool and after an exhausting interview process I was accepted. This was pretty amazing in and of itself as it was, and still is quite competitive to be accepted. I guess they believed in me before I believed in myself. We rented our house, packed up the horse trailer and moved to Seattle with two pre-school age girls.We didn't know anybody, and didn't have hardly any savings. I knew I could borrow the money and Kelly has always been a hard worker and will do whatever it takes to make things happen. I am not sure most people can comprehend how scary this was to leave a good paying job, go deep into debt, to pursue my passion. Not to mention all of the people that told me I was crazy for pursuing this and committing economic suicide. I only tell you all of this to lend some perspective regarding why I feel qualified to write this book. So 4 years later there I was, a newly minted Dentist.

Now I'm not sharing theory; I'm sharing survival. Fast forward 25+ years,when doctors diagnosed me with my health crisis, a rare blood disorder. I was told I could no longer practice Dentistry as the stress among other things would speed up the progression of my disease. They presented two paths: exist as a shadow of my former self or find a way to thrive despite it. The medication keeping me alive costs $500,000 annually—a number that would financially and psychologically crush most men. So once again I think most people would be devastated to have something they have worked so hard for taken away. Yet I'm not just functioning;

I'm enjoying wilderness experiences, coaching men to discover their inner badass, and writing this book while men half my age with the same condition can barely get out of bed.

This isn't about impressing you. It's about showing you what's possible when you apply anti-fragile principles to your own life. Every strategy in this book has been pressure-tested against real catastrophe—not just minor inconveniences. If these approaches can transform a potential death sentence into my most vital years, imagine what they can do for the challenges you're facing.

My motivation for writing this book is because I know firsthand that older men need some guidance regarding expectations for the future. The narrative around aging is mostly negative and focuses on the things that are "lost" as we get older. We focus on how good we used to be, and how life goes downhill after age 50, or even sooner in some instances.

The current narrative around aging and simply being a man that drives me crazy is that we must change, adapt, and, in some cases, feel bad about things we have done in the past as men in society. While it is good to learn from the past, it is *not* good to dwell on the past. The male contribution to the family unit and society as a whole is needed now more than ever! Don't let the "cancer" of a growing acceptance of a declining average become our reality. Complacency is not okay. Laziness is not okay. Apathy is not okay. Not taking care of our own mental and physical health is not okay. We must take responsibility for helping ourselves and others. We are the exception. Let's become hard to take down. As my hunter friends would say, "Be able to pack a lot of lead!"

BEYOND RESILIENCE: BECOMING UNSTOPPABLE

This book is your wake-up call, your battle cry, and your blueprint for becoming an unstoppable force in a world of constant change. It's not about just getting by or even bouncing back; it's about using every challenge as fuel for your personal evolution. You'll learn to see failure not as a roadblock but as a detour to even greater success. We also need to give ourselves some grace. This human "thing" is hard! We are, at the most basic level, meat-suits trying to do our best in this world we were thrown into.

We're going to rewire your brain to stop comparing yourself to others, especially those picture-perfect frauds on social media. You'll develop a love for yourself so deep that what others think becomes irrelevant. This book is your permission slip to become the man you've always had the potential to be - strong, adaptable, and unfazed by whatever life throws your way.

This isn't about proving your masculinity to anyone—it's about developing a version of manhood that serves you and those around you. The kind of masculinity that doesn't crumble under criticism or harden into rigidity but evolves and adapts while maintaining its core strength. It's about responsibility—literally your "ability to respond" to whatever comes your way.

There will be many ideas in this book that you have never heard of or possibly never even thought of. Don't view these ideas as gospel, but rather try them on like a new expensive pair of leather boots. You know the kind. I have a favorite pair that I have had for more than 35 years. Yup, the same pair of boots. But before you think, well, this guy just simply hasn't "used" these boots, let me tell you they have been used and even abused at times.

They are custom, hand-made boots built by a company in Spokane, Washington, named White's Boots. They are uncomfortable as hell when you first put them on, even though they are hand-made specifically to fit *your* feet. Who knew that our own two feet can greatly differ in size? It took about six months of wearing them pretty much every day until they became comfortable. I even wore them in water and let them dry on my feet to get an even more comfortable fit. I have sent them in a couple of times to get refurbished, but they are still amazingly comfortable after more than 35 years.

I think you will see life in a whole new light when you try on some of these brand new ideas, wear them around for a while, and give them enough time to break in.

I also want to give credit where credit is due. First and foremost,, I want to thank my father. Was he perfect? Hell no, but damn near! None of us are perfect, but he was/is my hero, even though he has been gone for years now. Did he just give me anything I wanted? Nope! But I never lacked anything I needed, and I learned so many valuable lessons from that man. Most of the lessons he taught me, I didn't even realize until years later.

I will always cherish the mentorship from men like Jim Rohn and Dr. Wayne Dyer, and Teddy Roosevelt in particular. These three guys were so far ahead of their time when it came to philosophies regarding thinking and living. I will be forever grateful for their wisdom and guidance. So it is with gratitude and appreciation that I have the privilege of sharing my thoughts, and theirs with you.

THIS ISN'T ANOTHER RESILIENCY BOOK

Being Antifragile doesn't mean you are simply more resilient. Being resilient by definition means being able to withstand or recover quickly from a difficult situation or being able to spring back into shape after bending, stretching, or being compressed. While these properties in humans can be noble, I am talking about so much more than that. While resilience is a good thing, it implies that there is the possibility of a breaking point sometime in the future.

On the other hand, Antifragile means a human being is not only resilient but also able to take adversity(wind), learn from it, and exit the storm on the other side even stronger.

The roots of a tree will grow deeper and wider when regularly subjected to strong winds, so even nature understands the

Antifragile concept. Most people back off in the face of adversity and begin to question themselves.

They start to think maybe they need to slow down or change course. Perhaps they decide it is not worth the effort. Maybe it was just a pipe dream anyhow and they wonder why they deserve whatever it was that they desired. But that way of thinking is toxic!

WHAT THIS BOOK IS NOT

Don't expect me to throw a bunch of research at you in this book. Most of us get bogged down by all that noise. And to top it off, half the research you see out there is cherry-picked to support someone's agenda. Lastly, many of the things we "knew" were true, but they turned out to be completely wrong. Remember how smoking was viewed in the 1950s?

For example, there is some research that could be helpful to contemplate. Consider this, a study in the British Medical journal in 2005 concluded this. If men retire early (55) they are 89% more likely to die in the 10 years after retirement than those that retire at 65. Interesting for sure.

However, over the course of a few decades, old boys like us have heard so much confusing stuff that we don't know what to believe and what *not* to believe. Coffee is bad; coffee is good. Eggs will kill you; eggs are the fountain of youth. While research is certainly welcome and necessary, I would rather distill this down into an actionable, easy-to-understand path forward to help *you*. Let's just cut through the noise and focus on what really matters—redefining what the rest of your life can and should look like and how to make it meaningful.

We tell ourselves we must be too old, have poor genetics, and so on. In reality we must understand that we are all different and all have different situations we are dealing with so give yourself some grace. If something isn't serving you then seek solutions. Just be careful with your reaction to the outcome.

These are *my* beliefs and *my* opinions about how to be an Antifragile Man. The principles I will discuss have not only been applied to and implemented by "yours truly" but also hundreds of clients. If you have a better way, then great, do that. However, I suspect you don't or you wouldn't be reading this book. I encourage you to keep an open mind because trial and error can be a great way forward. Progress is never a straight line.

Finally, it's important to note that under most circumstances, Antifragility only applies to animate objects. Inanimate objects really cannot get stronger as a result of adversity and chaos. If the glass shatters, as the saying goes, "too bad, so sad." For outdoorsmen like me, here is another way to look at it: My chainsaw does not get better as I cut more trees with it. *I* may get better and more efficient, but my saw? Not so much. Or how about my thousand-dollar fly Rod? What if you set it down next to you to have lunch on the streambank and your 1,400-pound horse who thinks he is a dog, comes over to see what's up and steps on it? Trust me when I say my fly-fishing rod is definitely *not* Antifragile. Ask me how I know.

Before we dive in, let me leave you with this last example of how Antifragility is so much more than just resilience. In ancient mythology, the Hydra was a beast so Antifragile that cutting off one head caused two more to grow in its place. That's the kind of unstoppable force you're about to become.

Are you ready to dive into the deep end? Let's get to work.

PART 1

AWAKEN THE ANTIFRAGILE MINDSET

CHAPTER 1

EMBRACING THE AGE OF WISDOM

When you reach the "back nine" of life, you face a crucial choice that few recognize: Will you merely age, or will you become antifragile? Never before in history have we been so blessed in every way, yet feel so anxious and uncertain about the future.

Social media has all of us purposely confused, because keeping us confused also keeps us searching for answers. What I've discovered through decades of medical practice and personal experience is a framework that transforms how we approach aging—one that doesn't just help you resist decline but actually leverages life's challenges to make you stronger.

Unlike fragile things that break under stress and resilient things that merely withstand stress, antifragile systems improve when challenged. Your aging body and mind can function this way too, but only if you recognize the opportunity.

You can choose to recognize and embrace the Antifragility you have nurtured over the years, rather than being a victim of aging.

The amazing thing is that it has been there all along; you just didn't recognize or appreciate it. You have a choice between the old path of victimhood or the new path of Antifragility. But here is the catch. The longer you go down the victim rabbit hole or simply coast into old age, the farther you get from the Antifragile badass you should have been. With the decision to embrace the wisdom from aging, you move toward the path of drastically slowing aging. One day in the near future, you may actually age backward, something called "longevity escape velocity," which we will discuss later.

WISDOM VERSUS KNOWLEDGE

To become antifragile, you must first understand a critical distinction that most people miss entirely: the difference between knowledge and wisdom.

- Knowledge is information you possess; wisdom is transformation you've experienced.

- Knowledge tells you that lifting weights builds muscle; wisdom is feeling stronger in every area of your life after six months of consistent training.

- Knowledge says inflammation causes disease; wisdom is experiencing the clarity that floods your mind when you eliminate inflammatory foods.

Too often, people try to learn only with their head. They consume information but never apply it in a way that transforms them. But when we connect knowledge with wisdom is where true growth and true Antifragility is born.

I'm not here to lecture you with studies and statistics, though I'll share some when relevant. Instead, I want to guide you through the same transformation I've witnessed in hundreds of patients who decided to become antifragile rather than accept decline. Rather, I want to share with you the wisdom I have gained through the gifts I have, knowing that in return you will share your gifts with me and the world, and then we can all get better together. A rising tide floats all of the boats.

My hope is that you won't just read this book but actually take action and make some decisions to change your life. Rather than just reading this book, I hope it stimulates you to ask yourself questions as well as provide some answers to those questions. It is better to read only one book per year and actually make meaningful changes, than to read 10 books a year and not apply any of the concepts that you learned.

Keep this in mind when you are thinking you have it so bad or life has not been fair. We need to really put this in perspective. If you are reading this book, you were likely born in the U.S. or have been here for a few years. You have already won the geographic lottery. Do you really have any idea how far ahead of the majority of the world's population you are? You have access to more gifts than almost any human ever to have walked the face of this earth.

Access to opportunity, food, shelter, safety, good paying jobs, and business opportunities, not to mention the holy grail of earthly gifts, freedom!

With all of that in mind, do you have the audacity to complain when your Starbucks coffee is too hot? Really? Many people have and will continue to die just trying to get into this country, willing to sacrifice everything. Trust me, most Americans aren't beating down the door or sacrificing everything to get into Mexico or, for that matter, most any other country on earth!. When you find yourself bitching about how bad you have it, please keep this top of mind and maintain the proper perspective.

WHAT IS THE PROPER PERSPECTIVE REGARDING AGING?

On one hand, we can buy into the narrative that aging sucks, that we are on a downhill slide, and we might as well accept that the door is going to hit us on the ass on the way out. This fragile approach to aging assumes that decline is inevitable, that retirement means retreat, and that your body and mind can only deteriorate from here. In this model, you become increasingly vulnerable to every stressor—a classic definition of fragility.

You've seen this fragile approach in action: men who retire and quickly deteriorate, both physically and mentally. They ponder if there's even a point in living anymore. They just want to sit on the couch, eat chips, and waste away. If that's what they want, then so be it. As long as they are "happy" with that lifestyle, then who are we to judge? Thriving and being a badass no matter your age is not for everybody, but if you had their defeatist attitude, you would not be reading this kind of book.

The antifragile approach to aging is fundamentally different. Rather than merely trying to prevent decline (resilience), you actively pursue growth by strategically exposing yourself to appropriate stressors. The science is clear: muscles, bones, cognitive function, and even immune responses strengthen when properly challenged. Notice that I only referenced a way of thinking and believing. There is a better way, and you have total control of the outcome! Simply stating that, believing that, and envisioning that (that YOU are in control) will produce radically different outcomes for you. If you embrace the fact that your life as you age can and will be amazing in every way, then it will be. That is the power of your mind.

This isn't merely positive thinking. The epigenetic research pioneered by Dr. Bruce Lipton in *The Biology of Belief* confirms that your mental state directly influences cellular function. When you combine this mindset with strategic physical practices, you create biological conditions that reverse many markers of aging.

If you practice this on a daily basis, things WILL happen in your life to support you. You don't really even need to know or figure out HOW to make your life amazing. If you simply believe it will be so, then things will be easier and better for you as a result. By simply being happy, cheerful, and hopeful, your life will become radically different from someone who believes "aging sucks." Yes, there will be ups and downs, "good" days and "bad" days, but the trajectory will always be up and to the right.

If you choose the victim mentality, the "aging sucks" mentality, you will continue to decline in vitality and go downhill, sometimes with alarming velocity. We have all seen examples of this. Consider the guy who spent his whole life "working for the man" and had his whole identity tied to that job. He was a good man with good intentions. He worked his ass off, and provided for his family and his basic needs but never really had any outside interests or things that fired him up. What happens when guys like this retire? Sadly, you know the answer: most of them are gone from this earth within a few years of retirement because they lacked purpose, didn't have any goals, and had a victim mentality.

An old adage says that the gifts we were given at birth are on loan from the Universe or God. We can continue to use them as long as we are using them to do good, help ourselves, and help others. However, if we are not using them, then they get recalled or recycled and given to someone else who will put them to good use. Although I am not a philosopher, I am, as I have said many times, a professional observer.

DO YOU CHOOSE HEALTH OR DISEASE?

Please keep your choice in mind. As I have said many times before, we don't really have a *health care* system in the United States, we have a *disease care* system. We have and continue to train the most advanced "health care" providers the world has ever seen. Please understand that I'm not here to berate any of our amazing healthcare practitioners who have spent their whole lives trying to help fellow human beings. Hell, I was one of them myself! The vast majority of these people have humanity's well-being at the forefront of everything that they do. However, if we truly look at the system we have in the United States, it's not a *health care* system; it is a *disease care* system.

We also have more recognized "specialties" in medicine than ever before. While this can be good, it also limits a practitioner from treating you holistically, or looking at all of the parts as belonging to a whole person. Currently, allopathic medicine treats different parts of the body as if they function independently, not as an intricately orchestrated, synergistic system. This couldn't be further from the truth. Everything is connected.

Our hospitals and primary care facilities are amazing at treating disease once it's already happened. Thank God we have them. I personally have been the beneficiary of many of their services over the years, and I would not be alive today without their expertise. The problem is that we are woefully behind in the *prevention* of disease. To compound this problem, we need to understand that pharmaceutical companies actually have a disincentive for people to be healthy and disease-free. Their system is set up to create drugs and procedures to help treat diseased individuals. Healthy individuals do not need the same level of healthcare as diseased individuals. Healthier people = less profit for them.

So how are we going to change this unhealthy reality? I suggest that the only way this is going to happen is if we create a community of like-minded people who are truly focused on prevention and wellness. We need a grassroots community that begins to think critically about these things and take action. Even if we educate ourselves as to how to stay well and still end up with some disease, we should go to our doctors and begin the narrative about how we could have prevented this in the first place and how we're going to heal this in the least invasive way.

We must undertake this change in taking our own health into our own hands for the sake of our kids, grandkids, great-grandkids, and, quite frankly, all of humanity.

With this in mind, I ask you, "Are you going to continue to watch the deterioration of our health as a society, or are you going to become a part of the solution?" I promise you that our overworked doctors would welcome any involvement from us. They are doing their best, but they are overwhelmed and buried in red tape and regulation. Change starts with *you* getting your own house in order, educating yourself, and then teaching others. I know we can begin a community here to inspire people to take control. Everybody wins, but we must take action.

ANTIFRAGILE TACTICS

- The choice of direction and mentality is yours. I suggest making this choice very carefully and very seriously. It doesn't need to be super complicated. There really are only about a half dozen things that, if you do them to the best of your ability, with intention, and consistently, will get you about 80 percent of the way toward your goals

- Are you going to be the exception, the one in your peer group that sets new expectations and inspires everyone around you, or are you going to attempt to bring others back down to embrace mediocrity? I love what Einstein said about this: "Great spirits have always encountered violent opposition from mediocre minds!" Chew on that for a while, and choose your side wisely. I suspect I will see you at the top if you're reading this book. It may not happen at the beginning, but it certainly will at the end. You need to share your gifts, the world needs you

I promise you that if you understand the principles in this book and take action, you will come up with a unique plan so that you can thrive and become Antifragile. Let's start with some definitions in the next chapter. I'll see you there.

CHAPTER 2

REDEFINING RETIREMENT AND PURPOSE

Let's get one thing straight: retirement isn't about trading in your boots for a pair of slippers and settling into a life of early bird specials. If that's your plan, this chapter isn't for you. But if you're the kind of guy who still has some fire in his belly, wants to kick open a few more saloon doors, and still chase the next adventure, then you're in the right place.

Here's what I've noticed: men who thrive in retirement don't just retire FROM something—they retire TO something. The difference is crucial. One approach leaves you hollowed out, the other makes you Antifragile.

This chapter is going to redefine what retirement means. It's not the end of the road but a new beginning—a time to reimagine purpose, identity, and how you want to spend the next chapter of your life. I don't have all the answers, and I'm not going to pretend to. What I do know is that the outdated notion of retirement as quietly riding off into the sunset needs to be re-imagined. We're going to talk about what it really means to stay engaged, purposeful, and thriving as you age.

WHAT SHOULD THIS LAST PHASE OF YOUR LIFE LOOK LIKE?

I have read some books about retirement that make me want to lose my lunch. These books talk about subjects as awful as homeowner's association (HOA) boards, the most comfortable slip-on shoes, the best 10-dollar meals, ED medications, and the latest pickleball strategy. (Sorry, my pickleball-loving friends.) These books assume decline. They're written from the perspective that your best days are behind you. That's not just depressing; it's dangerous.

It also drives me crazy to hear older men talking about the "good old days." First of all, you were likely not really that good back then, or at least not as good as you remember. It is sad to listen to some guys still talking about their high school football game where they scored the winning touchdown. Nobody really cares. People would rather know what you have done recently. If you were really that good, then understand that guy is still there inside you. He's just a little beaten up from living life. Rather than focus on how good you used to be and the loss of that, focus on the lessons you have learned since then and how good you are now as a result of that wisdom.

This backward fixation violates the first principle of becoming Antifragile in retirement, which is that you must be future-oriented while living in the present.

My people want to saddle up, gallop wide open through every saloon door, pour back a shot of whiskey, and haul ass back outside bound for places unknown with a big ol' smile on their face. They want to climb a mountain, run whitewater on a river, jump out of a perfectly good airplane, sign up for a Spartan race, or hike the Grand Canyon.

Being Antifragile in retirement isn't just about adrenaline, however. It's about intentionally seeking challenges that force you to grow stronger. Some days, that's a mountain climb. Other days, it's mastering a new skill or building deeper relationships. The common thread is that you're constantly testing your boundaries rather than protecting your comfort.

After all, what do we have to lose? Remember, you are an old guy. Life is not a dress rehearsal, and the last time I checked, there are no luggage racks on a hearse. Sorry, but you can't take it with you.

Retirement is not the end; it's your next mission. I consider it your new beginning. It is a special time where you can finally take all of the lessons you have learned through years of being "lifed-on" and formulate a plan that feeds your soul.

HOW WE BELIEVE RETIREMENT OR THE NEXT CHAPTER WILL CHANGE OUR LIVES

In my quest to make this book valuable *and* actionable, I interviewed many people from various backgrounds. Many of the things they were excited about and the things they were concerned about were similar, and some were unique to their particular situation. Here is a partial list.

"What are you excited about regarding retirement?"

1. Time freedom

2. Time to spend traveling

3. Time to spend with family, especially parents and grandchildren

4. Time to pursue hobbies (golf, fishing, reading)

5. Pursuing outdoor interests

6. Volunteering

7. Celebrating the wisdom gained over the years

8. Having a flexible schedule (or no schedule)

9. Mentoring younger kids

10. Decreased stress.

"What are you apprehensive about in retirement?"

1. Financial security (an overwhelming concern for most respondents)

2. Declining health

3. Losing identity/social connection

4. They will miss the thrill of pursuit or feeling of accomplishment from their job

5. They will miss the travel required that was paid for by their company

6. Lost sense of purpose and productivity

7. Lost mental stimulation

8. Fear that more time with a spouse could negatively affect the relationship

Looking at these lists, do you notice something? Nearly all the positives are about what you'll gain—time, freedom, and flexibility. Nearly all the negatives are about what you'll lose—identity, purpose, connection. This reveals a fundamental truth: how you experience retirement depends entirely on whether you view it through the lens of addition or subtraction.

It's important to point out that the reason you might be stressed about getting older is that you don't have a plan. When you have a plan and a clear path ahead, life becomes easier, more enjoyable, and more predictable, eliminating the stress you feel over it. But not just any plan. You need an Antifragile plan—one that doesn't just survive the challenges of aging but actually gets better because of them.

Let's come up with a plan or at least begin to think about that. Remember that discomfort or uneasiness is there to help you by making you search for solutions. Discomfort should not be seen as any sort of punishment.

Whenever you feel uncomfortable, see that feeling as an opportunity to grow back even stronger. Discomfort and the like are there to help you improve upon some of the areas in your life that aren't exactly as you want them to be. Rather than try to avoid discomfort anytime it shows up, embrace it as something you need to learn and conquer.

INCREASE YOUR HEALTHSPAN, NOT JUST YOUR LIFESPAN BY BEING PRESENT

I have heard pushback over the years regarding living longer. Remarks like, "Why would I want to live longer?" When I dig deeper, what they're really saying is, "I don't want more years of decline and dependency." Who would? I think comments like this are very misinformed. I understand people's thinking around not really wanting to live a long life because often we see older people as weak, grumpy, dependent, and basically living a pretty sad existence. But what if we could begin to look at being older as still being vibrant and useful?

In my view of living a longer, more fulfilled life, one must distinguish between *lifespan* and *health-span*—two drastically different things. Lifespan refers to the actual quantity of years lived. Healthspan refers to the quantity *and* quality of your years on earth. An Antifragile retirement focuses relentlessly on healthspan. Every decision you make should be filtered through the question: "Will this help me stay vital, engaged, and independent longer?" My definition of a fulfilled life is to be happy and useful right up until the end. Think about this quote.

> *"If you are depressed, you're living in the past,*
> *and if you're anxious, you're living in the future."*
> —*Brianna Wiest, The Mountain is You*

One of the best ways to increase our *health-span* is simply by staying present. The past and future only truly exist in our minds. The present is the only reality. If you feel anxious or depressed, all you need to do is focus on right here, right now.

EMBRACE EXCITEMENT, NOT FEAR

Imagine the potential shift in our perceptions of old age. What if we quit fearing death and realized that it is an inevitable reality for mortal beings? Remember, just being born is a terminal illness. Rather than fearing death, we should fear the potentially devastating consequences of not living a meaningful life while we are here. The tragedy isn't dying; it's dying with potential still untapped, adventures still untaken, and wisdom still unshared. With this in mind, we should reconsider our perception of living longer.

What is your view of retirement and aging right now? I encourage you to put this book down and write down five (or more) things you are excited about in retirement and five (or more) things you are apprehensive about. Conduct this exercise with your significant other, or possibly do it separately and then compare notes. This is a valuable exercise for everyone to contemplate. Now set your answers aside, and we will revisit them near the end of the book.

ANTIFRAGILE TACTICS

- Retirement isn't a finish line; it's a launchpad for your next adventure. Forget the outdated idea of quietly fading into the background. This is the time to reimagine your purpose and embrace new challenges

- Focus on *healthspan* over lifespan. It's not just about how many years you live but about living those years with vitality and purpose. You don't have to settle for a slow decline into old age. You can—and should—stay vibrant, useful, and engaged right up until the end

- Having a plan eliminates stress. A lack of direction in retirement can create anxiety. When you define a clear path, everything becomes more enjoyable, manageable, and less stressful.

- Embrace discomfort as an opportunity to grow stronger. This is Antifragility! If you feel uneasy or uncertain about retirement or aging, that discomfort can guide you toward areas in your life that need improvement. Instead of fearing it, see it as a tool for growth

- The present is all we have. Don't get lost in thinking about the "good old days" or worrying about the future. Focus on making the most of right now. Your greatest asset is the wisdom you've accumulated; use it to shape what comes next

- Stop retiring *from* something and start retiring *to* something. The difference between these mindsets is the difference between decline and growth

- Redefine what aging looks like for you. Being older doesn't have to mean being frail or dependent. You can change your mindset and live a vibrant life by shifting how you think about aging and retirement

- Identify what excites you and what worries you about the next phase of your life or retirement. Take the time to sit down and list your hopes and concerns about the next chapter of your life. This will help guide you toward building a life that is fulfilling and aligned with your true desires

Conventional retirement plans prepare you to weather storms. An Antifragile retirement plan ensures you come out of those storms stronger than you went in.

CHAPTER 3

NAVIGATING MODERNITY

Let's face it: life today is a lot like walking into a diner and being handed a 20-page menu. There are so many options, so many temptations, and you just want something that won't require Pepto Bismol later.

Modern life bombards us with an endless stream of "solutions" promising to make us healthier, happier, and more productive. But here's the uncomfortable truth: most of these quick fixes are making us weaker, not stronger. While everyone else is frantically downloading the latest productivity app or jumping on another 30-day challenge, what if you could build something more valuable—a life that actually thrives under pressure?

We're all trying to hack our way to success, but more often than not, those shortcuts turn into wild goose chases. Whether it's our health, relationships, or that shiny new piece of tech that promises to make life easier but ends up causing headaches, we're all guilty of looking for the quick fix.

By nature, humans are always looking for the easy way out. Remember high school geometry? The shortest distance between points "A" and "B" was a straight line (that may also be the only thing I remember from high school geometry).

This obsession with shortcuts isn't new, but it's never been more dangerous than it is today. The modern world has created a perfect storm where our ancient biological programming collides with technological conveniences that offer instant gratification. We're left with the illusion of control while becoming increasingly fragile.

But here's the thing: the quick fixes we rely on in life—whether it's for our health, navigating technology, or dealing with social media—are actually holding us back. In this chapter, I will show you how understanding the real challenges we face today can help you take control, improve your well-being, and avoid the traps everyone else is falling into.

QUICK FIXES AREN'T QUICK…OR FIXES

We've all fallen for it before—the promise that one breakthrough, the new diet, the new workout plan, or one magic solution will solve everything. Whether it's a pill, a new gadget, or the latest fitness trend, we can't resist the idea that everything can be fixed overnight. But what's the reality? It's a bit more complicated.

One of the greatest examples of this was the Human Genome Project. The overarching concept was that if we could elucidate all of the human genes through gene sequencing, we would have the "cure" for any ailment.

Consequently, in the 1990s, private and governmental money was given to scientists to figure this out. It took nine years to sequence the first single gene! It took another four years to sequence the rest of the total of 46 chromosomes, consisting of 23 pairs. Voila! The fountain of youth is open for business, you can break out the swim trunks!

Well, we may have a problem here, Houston. It turns out there were a few missing details. First, there is something called epigenetics. Now, before your eyes glaze over and you start scrolling through the channels looking for reruns of *Gunsmoke*, it is an interesting concept.

Epigenetics revealed that our genes aren't our destiny—they're more like potential that may or may not be expressed depending on how we live our lives. In other words, the instruction manual for your body isn't written in permanent ink; it's constantly being edited by your environment, behaviors, and choices.

By definition, epigenetics is "The study of organisms caused by modification of gene expression rather than alteration of the genetic code itself." Okay, well, what the hell does that mean to regular guys like us? It means that you can stop the expression of a gene, even if you have a certain genetic code for some trait, if you incorporate different aspects of behavior and environmental factors into your daily life.

In other words, if you eat certain foods, get enough movement, lift a few heavy things, get the right amount of sleep, and avoid certain "toxic" environments (both mental and physical), that gene may never get the chance to express itself. It is like a light switch that never gets turned on.

This is tremendous news because it means that we are not idle bystanders waiting for "the shoe to drop." We have control! For example, even if you carry the 9P21 genotype dubbed "the heart attack gene," if you adopt certain lifestyle principles and get the proper medical care, you will never need to suffer from a heart attack (or stroke).

"WHY EVEN BOTHER?"

How many times have you heard men say, "Well, I am probably gonna die from a heart attack because my daddy did at age 55, and two of my uncles did too," or some such thing? I mean, why adopt a healthy lifestyle if you are going to croak soon anyhow? Hell, why not just eat whatever you want, forget about any exercise or preventive behaviors, and just live it up?

This fatalistic thinking—a surrender to perceived inevitability—is the exact opposite of antifragility. It assumes we're fragile machines running predetermined software rather than adaptive organisms designed to respond to our environment.. Now you know that it doesn't have to be an inevitable downward trend if you learn more, think differently, and take action. You have control, but you must *take* control. The one thing those pessimistic men all had in common was that they probably had the same things in their refrigerator and pantry, and had the same favorite football team. The good news is that you can control what food you eat.

Knowledge without action is useless. Understanding that your genes aren't your destiny means nothing if you don't leverage that information by making different choices than your ancestors did.

Consistent small stresses make us stronger than searching for perfect protection. The small stresses of regular exercise, intermittent fasting, temperature variation, and even certain mental challenges prevent decline and strengthen our biological systems. The body adapts positively to appropriate stress but deteriorates with either too much stress or none at all.

But the implications of epigenetics go far beyond just disease prevention. It challenges our entire approach to health in modernity. We've been trained to think that health comes from outside interventions—from doctors, pills, and procedures. The reality? Your body is designed to thrive when given the right conditions, many of which have been part of human existence for millennia: natural foods, physical activity, social connection, mental challenges, and environmental variety.

The Human Genome Project and the study of Epigenetics also pointed out something else that was quite interesting. Did you know (I didn't) that we as humans have more bacterial DNA than we do human DNA? It is estimated that we have about 30 trillion human cells and 38 trillion bacterial cells. These cells work in concert with our bodies to keep us alive and well.

Our obsession with cleanliness and convenience has made us more vulnerable, not less. By attempting to eliminate all sources of discomfort and "contamination" from our lives, we've inadvertently weakened the very systems designed to protect us.

Most people think we need to nuke all of the bacteria. For the most part, they are our friends. In fact, we would die without them in our body. For the purposes of this book we won't get into the weeds on this but I wanted you to at least know this.

You don't need to be the sharpest knife in the drawer to understand the implications of this. We need to rethink all of this hand sanitizer, clean-freak stuff that we have come to accept as "good" for us. If I put on my Dentist hat here for a bit, don't even get me started on excessive use of mouthwash. Suffice it to say it is *not* a good idea to get rid of all of the bacteria in your mouth on a daily basis unless you have severe "Gum" disease and even then, you need a specific plan to nuke only the "bad actors".

Consider how our ancestors were exposed to thousands of microbial species daily through soil, fermented foods, and close contact with other humans and animals. Their immune systems were constantly training against a diverse array of challenges. Modern sanitation has saved countless lives from deadly pathogens, but the pendulum has swung too far, leaving us with immune systems that are undertrained and misguided—leading to skyrocketing rates of allergies, autoimmune conditions, and chronic inflammation.

That is not to say that all bacteria are good. There are some bad actors out there for sure, but we need to keep things in perspective. Think about this when you are obsessive with hand sanitizers and mouthwashes too, especially with young kids whose immune systems are still developing. Always consider risk vs. benefit when using antibiotics. You may nuke a few bad bugs, but you may also take out some of your buddies (the good bacteria) with friendly fire along the way.

DIGITAL DEPENDENCY: THE INVISIBLE FRAGILITY

Another challenge we face today is the instant and abundant availability of technology, particularly social media. Technology has created a paradox in our lives. We've never been more connected, yet never more isolated; never had more information, yet never been more confused; never had more conveniences, yet never felt more stressed. Convenience often creates hidden vulnerabilities.

While we marvel at how easily children navigate digital interfaces, we're overlooking something crucial: their facility with these tools isn't developing alongside other fundamental skills—it's replacing them. A child who can download an app but can't tie their shoes represents a new kind of fragility.

Aren't navigation aids these days absolutely mind-blowing? We can type in the address of somewhere we want to go and within seconds the route is figured out for us. The device even tells us how long it should take to get there, and gives us alternate routes!

Today's sophisticated navigation systems are a far cry from the old days of stopping at the 7-11 and asking the store clerk for directions for you to write on your partially used McDonald's napkin. There are even apps for navigation in the backcountry now, places you have never been. You can even download the map ahead of time if you'll be without cell service.

I defiantly asked my high school math teacher one day why I had to learn to do math longhand and show my work. His confident response was, "Well, my son, you can't just walk around with a calculator in your pocket all day." Well, Mr. Jones, I guess you got that one wrong.

And "Google?" Are you kidding me? That was what all the nerds did to the girls at the high school prom, except me, of course. I was "cool." Today, you can just ask Siri, Google, or Chat GPT anything you want, and they have the answer. Man, I could have used that in school!

Years ago, if I traveled out of town without my wife, which was rare, it was always a bit awkward going out to dinner by myself. I could just imagine what other people thought, looking at me sitting there by myself. "Oh, honey, look at that poor guy over there all by himself! He must be a real loser or maybe a sociopathic serial killer."

I have always wanted to make a T-shirt that says, "I have a beautiful wife and children, but I'm here on business," or something really cool like that. Enter the cell phone. Now I can look like I have something really important to do while I am having dinner by myself. Indeed, because I am so important, it requires my immediate attention. Hell, I can even pretend I am talking to someone really important.

Cell phones have changed everything socially. Some of it is good, and some of it is bad. Whatever happened to getting to know the other solo diner who is also there alone sitting next to you? How about starting up an old-fashioned conversation with them?

After putting down my phone and engaging with the other person next to me, I have had some of the most amazing conversations. It is amazing how we are all connected in some way. I always learn something, usually something I had never even thought of. Who knew that the research shows that there is not enough lithium available on earth to make enough batteries to power all of the electric cars we would need if everyone chose electric?

Yup, I learned that from a research geologist who was sitting next to me the other evening at a local restaurant. The point is, use the phone for all of its wonderful purposes, and then put the damn thing down and talk to people. You will find it fascinating. It may even help you add another arrow to your Antifragility quiver.

Another place where cell phones have changed the landscape is at the gym. Back in the day, the gym was a social place where everyone knew everyone and encouraged each other. A lot of my best friends came from the gym. Today, everyone has their headphones in and most barely make eye contact.

Now, I hear you saying, "Well, I am listening to my favorite podcast or motivational music." That is great, but occasionally, look up, maybe smile, take out the earpiece, and say hello. You can develop amazing relationships because these people are on the same journey as you. Your ancient DNA craves connection. After all, that is what kept the whole tribe alive way back then.

Just don't take my advice to the opposite extreme, either. Don't be the old guy who talks endlessly about your recently developed hemorrhoids, sore shoulder, or something similar. People are busy and don't need to hear about all of your problems. Only you and occasionally your doctor really care about those things. We all have enough of our own issues to deal with.

One last thing regarding technology. It could be making us one of the most vulnerable generations that ever existed. We have all witnessed what can happen after a hurricane or other catastrophic event. The power goes out, along with cell towers, cell phone service, communication, and the internet.

Some people are totally lost and helpless. I saw reports on the evening news that some folks didn't know how to get to the grocery store to get essentials because their navigation app didn't work. *Are you kidding me?* These are the same folks who likely do not know where the milk comes from in the first place.

Imagine if something like this happened on a widespread level. At that point, the Hazda people in Tanzania would be better able to survive and thrive because they would know how to get their own food and water, stay warm, and be self-sufficient. So ask yourself, are we really all that advanced and Antifragile, or are we so fragile that if the power goes out, we panic?

I am not implying anything about you personally, but I am asking you to reflect on how durable you are if things go south.

CARTELS AND FRUIT SALADS

Years ago, I brought in a guest speaker to one of our dental conventions to talk about drug use in our high schools. This guy was the head of the DEA for New York and was responsible for bringing down one of the most prolific drug cartels ever.

These folks were no joke, so this was a big deal, and this guy was the real deal. I remember him telling me that he was disappointed when he heard the "price on his head" was so low because he thought he was a bigger deal than that. Anyhow, it was fascinating to look at his approach to helping young kids.

The day before he was speaking, he would come to the town and go to the local high school. He would ask the principal to identify 20 kids with various skill sets and backgrounds (yes, he was inclusive) to meet with him that afternoon. Once gathered in a room, he would assure them that what they said in that room stayed in that room (kind of like Vegas), and their "secrets" were safe with him.

After gaining their trust, he would ask them what the drug scene was like in that tiny Montana school. I was blown away to hear what was going on in our peaceful little town. He shared no names or specific instances, but real stories nonetheless.

I always thought a fruit salad was something grandma brought to the potluck on Sunday, but boy was I wrong. I learned a "fruit salad" was where all the kids would bring some pills from the medicine chest at home and throw them in a bowl. Because most prescription meds are different colors so that they can be identified, the bowl was full of a lot of different colors.

When all the pills were thrown in there, the kids would take a handful and wait to see what happened. Needless to say, this is *crazy* dangerous.

So how did the kids know which pills to steal? The ones that had labels with "do not operate machinery" or "do not drink alcohol while taking these" (or something similar), were considered the "good" ones to put in the fruit salad. To top it off, there are many more similar stories just like this. Let's be fair and say that most kids are good kids and know better, but we need to get a handle on all of this!

There were many valuable lessons here. First, you may think that *your* kids and grandkids would never do that in your Mayberry-like community, but are you sure? I think you need to be aware of where meds are stored and educate your kids and grandkids. Talk to them.

I think the most valuable lesson I learned was that when I asked the DEA agent what the single best thing we can do as adults to help with all of these problems, he said without hesitation, "Eating dinner together as a family with no cell phones at the table." I said, "What? That's all you can say about this?"

He relayed to me that the single most powerful predictor of whether your kids and grandkids will fall into this trap or others was simple: eating dinner together with no cell phones. Seriously? That's it? It seems easy enough to do, so use that as food for thought. Remember, they watch everything we do, so we need to be Antifragile *and* a good role model. Let's help these young men and lead by example. Their life can literally hang in the balance.

Social media, modern devices and other technology can be extremely useful, *and* extremely harmful. With the rise of A.I. and other tech exploding, I just want you to give it some thought and set some guardrails around how you use these new technologies.

ANTIFRAGILE TACTICS

- Beware of "quick fixes"

- Put the cell phone down occasionally and connect with people(especially during mealtime)

- Lead by example, others are watching you

- Beware of the risks and benefits from incorporating Technology in your life and set some guardrails (rules of engagement)

Now we've discussed the age of wisdom, redefining "retirement", and some technological and modern challenges. Next, it's time to start applying our learning to the concept of Antifragility. I'll see you in Part 2.

MENTAL REPROGRAMMING FOR ANTI-FRAGILITY

OVERCOMING LIMITING BELIEFS: HOW DO ANTIFRAGILE MEN THINK AND ACT?

When Nassim Taleb coined the term "antifragile," he described something fundamentally different from resilience. While resilient things resist damage and stay the same, antifragile things actually get better when exposed to stressors, volatility, and chaos. Like your muscles growing after the stress of weightlifting, an antifragile mindset turns life's challenges into fuel for growth. This chapter explores how men in their final third of life can develop this rare and powerful quality.

As funny as it may sound, we are born with only two fears: the fear of falling and the fear of loud sounds. *Any* other fears have been taught to us by well-meaning parents or loved ones, or have we just decided to be fearful of something because of some experience we had? I find all of the fears people have these days fascinating. Fear of an empty nest, lack of money, losing your identity/purpose, boredom, death of friends/loved ones, your own death, injury/sickness, Alzheimer's, and on and on. Most forms of fear are due to our limiting beliefs.. Remember the list of things you are apprehensive about in this last phase of life that I asked you to think about and write down? Pull that list out now, and let's reframe some of those fears or apprehensions.

As men age, society often expects decline, caution, and gradual withdrawal. But what if aging could be your superpower rather than your kryptonite? The antifragile approach flips conventional wisdom: each health challenge becomes an opportunity to optimize your remaining systems, each relationship loss deepens your appreciation for connection, and each forced adaptation makes you more mentally flexible than younger men trapped in rigid thinking patterns.

In this chapter, we explore the concept of Antifragility and how recognizing and overcoming our limiting beliefs can transform us from fragile to Antifragile. We'll learn how to turn adversity into strength and use our perceived setbacks as wisdom gained, not "bad" things or setbacks. By the end of this chapter, you'll understand how to cultivate an Antifragile mindset that will serve you well in the final third of your life.

ARE FEARS WISDOM?

Let's delve into this concept of fears, limiting beliefs, and perceived setbacks. We should view these things as wisdom gained, not bad things or setbacks. Instead of viewing your scars as a symbol of the bad things that have happened to you, use your scars to reinforce your badassedness. Scars prove to the world that you do not sit on the sidelines and watch. *You* get in the game, possibly get beat down, and literally become stronger as a result of that. We win or we learn (but we never fail), and we persevere until we get it right. That is how an Antifragile man sees the world.

So what does an Antifragile man look like and how does he conduct himself? My first observation of an Antifragile man goes back to Teddy Roosevelt. I have his "Man in the Arena" quote plastered all over my offices. If you have never seen it or read it recently, I suggest you look it up. Pay attention to the words. The speech it belongs to is one of my favorites of all time. I have read nearly all of his books and those written about him. Hell, I even named my black and white Paint-Percheron cross gelding after him!

Roosevelt exemplified antifragility in how he transformed his childhood asthma and physical weakness into motivation for his legendary "strenuous life." When his first wife and mother died on the same day, he channeled his grief into more determined public service. As he aged, his adventurous spirit only grew stronger— leading expeditions into uncharted territories in his later years when most men were settling into rocking chairs.

Sidenote: he *hated* being called "Teddy." A well-meaning man conjured up the name, but "Teddy" hated the implication. In 1902, "Teddy" was on a hunting trip when a guide named Collier cornered and stunned a bear for Roosevelt to shoot. "Teddy" was appalled by the idea of shooting a bear that he hadn't pursued himself. A *Washington Post* journalist named, Clifford Berryman created a cartoon depicting the incident, and it became a national sensation. Subsequently, a New York store owner heard the story, made a stuffed bear, and named it the "Teddy" bear. The "Teddy" bear was born, but "Teddy" actually preferred to be called Colonel or Mr. President.

The Antifragile man will use annoyances to his advantage, not see them as problems. Becoming Antifragile means taking these perceived problems or setbacks, applying the wisdom we have acquired over the years, and crushing those previously held beliefs. Rather than shrinking back into our fears, we double down on our resolve to overcome and thrive in these environments. It really is just a decision—when we recognize fear or anxiety rearing its ugly head, we say to ourselves "oh hell no" and run right through the previously perceived brick wall. Antifragile Men always have more than one option. We are masters when it comes to problem-solving.

Here's a real-life Antifragile example: I was at a conference in Austin, Texas, with other thought leaders hell-bent on making a difference in the world. One night at about 1:00 A.M., I awoke to a loud banging sound and heard one hell of a wind blowing. I found the door to the outside deck area had blown wide open.

Debris was flying everywhere, and rain was soaking the floor. The cushions on the couch outside blew by me on their way to Florida, I believe.

There I was in my underwear, trying to get the door closed, working against the wind. I had to pull at it with all my strength. Finally, I thought, "Okay, mission accomplished," but when I let go, it blew wide open again. I soon realized that the latch on the door had malfunctioned, and it was not going to be an easy fix. I am pretty sure most guys would have called the maintenance crew, but I just didn't want to bother them at that hour of the morning. Besides, they had many "issues" to contend with during this nasty storm.

What to do? I looked around and surmised the belts off of the hotel's bathrobes would double nicely as a rope to tie to a chair inside the room to keep the door closed. I tell you this story to demonstrate that sometimes we just need to figure shit out ourselves, not call someone to our rescue every time we get in a jam. Antifragile at its finest hour!

This small example illustrates a crucial truth for aging men: the more we outsource our problems to others—whether that's calling maintenance for every household issue or immediately turning to doctors for every ache—the more dependent and fragile we become. Antifragility demands that we continue to exercise our problem-solving muscles, especially as we age. The less we use these capabilities, the faster they deteriorate.

The lesson here is that having one option makes you fragile, a couple of options makes you a bit less fragile, but unlimited options makes you an Antifragile force to be reckoned with. Like the old saying goes: either lead, follow, or get the hell out of the way!

HOW SHOULD WE VIEW AGING?

If we continue to see aging as a disability, it will continue to be a disability. Let's blow that shit up! As I have said, just being born is a terminal illness, so get over it and savor every day!

The revolutionary power of this mindset shift cannot be overstated, and remarkably, science backs it up. Your beliefs about aging literally determine how you age—not just emotionally but physically.

Let me introduce a brilliant study that was done to drive home this point. You may think that you don't have any limiting beliefs. You may not believe that mindset matters and that your beliefs really don't matter. You are an "it is what it is" kind of guy. Let's look at what was dubbed the counter-clockwise study, done by Ellen Langer in 1979.[2] This lady is truly a pioneer. In 1981, she was the first woman ever to be tenured in Psychology at Harvard University.

She designed her study brilliantly. In 1979, she enrolled men in their seventies. She rented a house for a week with the goal

---

[2] Langer, Ellen. Counterclockwise: Mindful Health and the Power of Possibility. Ballantine Books, 2009

of recreating an environment similar to what the men would have lived in circa 1959. Right from the beginning, the men had to conduct themselves as if they were younger. She set the precedent right in the beginning that these men had to envision that they *were* younger, just like they would have been in 1959. For example, they had to carry their own suitcases or leave them behind. There were no reminders of their actual age, and there were not even any mirrors in the house where they could see themselves. The newspapers (remember those?), magazines, movies, and books were all period-specific. Hell, even the TV was black and white. These men were even instructed to dress like they would have back then, and the only pictures were of themselves or their families back in 1959.

The results were staggering. By every metric, these men aged backward and appeared younger at the end, even after only one week! Many of the men showed up to the house on day one using walkers or canes to assist them while walking, but by the end, they all walked out of the house on their own accord.

Even later, when independent researchers evaluated before and after pictures of the men, not knowing which was which, they all reported that the men even looked younger when they left the house versus when they first arrived. What's even more important is that after checking back in with these men or their families 20 years later, they found that those who adopted a more positive outlook on aging lived on average 7 ½ years longer than those who looked at aging as a negative thing. Not a bad return on investment, especially considering the fact that the positive people lived the additional years healthy, happy, fulfilled, and most assuredly vibrant.

Think about what this means for you right now. The very act of reading this book—of engaging with ideas that frame aging as an opportunity for growth rather than decline—could potentially add years to your life. But more importantly, it adds life to your years.

The most profound implication of Langer's study isn't just that positive thinking helps—it's that our cultural narratives about aging are actively harmful. Every time you accept the notion that "senior moments" are inevitable, that decline is normal, that you're "too old" for new adventures, you're programming your body and brain for deterioration.

What if we approached aging not as something to fight against or resign ourselves to but as a unique phase with its own advantages? What if the loss of youthful physical prowess creates space for deeper wisdom, more meaningful relationships, and a more carefully curated life?

KICK LIMITING BELIEFS TO THE CURB

Now, let's talk about limiting beliefs specifically. What are those, and how do we know we have them? A limiting belief is a state of mind or a belief that restricts you in some way. These are formed between 0 and 7 years old. Yes, zero, since even before we are born, our mothers' beliefs influence us. It is important to understand that moms are usually well-meaning, and they are trying to protect you from disappointment, but these beliefs can be devastating if you do not begin to recognize them.

For men entering their final third of life, these early limiting beliefs combine with society's negative messaging about aging to create a double burden. The childhood belief that "I'm not good enough" merges with the cultural belief that "older men are irrelevant" to produce a particularly toxic mindset.

Limiting beliefs come from your brain's desire (and your parents' desire) to protect you and help you avoid pain in the future. Did you ever hear your parents or adults you looked up to say things like these?

- Money is bad

- I don't have enough time

- I don't have enough experience

- I'm too old/ too young

- I'm not talented enough

- I'm not smart enough

- That's not for people like us

- I am terrible at public speaking

This list could go on and on. These beliefs don't come from reality; they come from a place of fear. Like it or not, we all have them. The key is to identify these unfounded beliefs and blow them up. Realize that we are all created equal and we all have talents and gifts that come naturally and easily to us, but there is *nothing* you cannot achieve if you understand this. Just remember this: if somebody else has already done it, then so can you with enough hard work and perseverance, but it all begins with believing that you can!

I can hear some of you saying, "Well, I'm 80 years old and never trained a day in my life, but I want to win the New York Marathon!" Then maybe you need to dial that back a bit and set a goal to *finish* a marathon first. If that is truly what you want and you are willing to do the work and get proper coaching, then I encourage you to do it.

Human beings are amazing creatures and can do astounding things, but it all starts with believing that you can. Take Roger Bannister as an example. He was an elite runner, and all of the "experts" said that a sub 4-minute mile was impossible for a human. In fact, people had been trying for at least 50 years. But once Bannister broke the perceived sub 4-minute barrier, just 46 days later, John Landry broke Bannister's record. In fact, in the next 3 years, 16 runners broke the sub 4-minute mile pace. So, do you still think your thoughts and beliefs don't matter?

We need to understand that all beliefs are useful but not necessarily true. There is a concept called epistemic humility. By definition, it is the ability to understand that you do not know everything and honestly accept that everything you *think* you know could be wrong. It is imperative that you understand this and apply this attitude to your own life and thinking. We have all heard the old saying that "you don't know what you don't know," but this takes it a step further to imply that maybe you don't even know what you thought you knew.

This kind of talk can start to confuse a regular guy like me, so let's look at some real-world applications. When you were a kid, you likely believed in Santa Claus. I sure did. Well, was it true? Was he real? I think we all know the answer to that, but was that belief useful? It was if it brought you and your family joy and hopefully it encouraged you to be nice and not naughty.

As a dentist, I fielded a lot of questions about the "tooth fairy." Many children asked if she really existed. The answer is no, but was she useful? Well, if she traded teeth that were now useless into cash, then yes, she was useful. How about when you were a kid riding around on the Stingray bike and you crashed and got an "owie?" If your Mom offered to kiss it and make it better, that was probably not true, but you believed it would help, so it was useful. I think you get the point here.

The following are the 7 steps to crush any limiting beliefs:

1. Ask yourself if the belief is true or not

2. Determine the source of the belief

3. Make a declaration like, "I do not believe this anymore."

4. Imagine what it will be like to shed that belief

5. Replace it with a belief that better serves you

6. Find evidence to validate the new belief

7. Observe the result (Do you feel/behave differently now?)

ANTIFRAGILE TACTICS

- Here's a quick Antifragile strategy to wrap up this chapter:

- Recognize that most fears are learned, not innate

- View setbacks as opportunities for growth and wisdom

- Strive to be like Teddy Roosevelt's "Man in the Arena"

- Identify and challenge your limiting beliefs

- Understand that these beliefs were often formed in childhood by well-meaning adults

- Believe in your ability to achieve, just like others have before you

- Practice epistemic humility—be open to the possibility that what you think you know could be wrong

- Remember that beliefs can be useful even if they're not necessarily true

- Use the 7 steps to uninstall beliefs that do not serve you

Now that we've explored how to recognize and overcome our limiting beliefs, let's dive deeper into some of the internal obstacles that can still hold us back, even after we've addressed these surface-level beliefs. In the next chapter, we'll tackle imposter syndrome, self-sabotage, and how our money mindset impacts success.

CHAPTER 5

IMPOSTER SYNDROME, SELF-SABOTAGE, AND MONEY MINDSET

Ask any über successful person if they have ever had imposter syndrome. I assure you 100 percent of them will say yes. Yes, even Oprah, all the presidents, the world leaders, Kobe, Reba, and Mother Teresa. All of them have had imposter syndrome at one time or another. When you feel like a fraud despite your accomplishments, you're experiencing what psychologists call imposter syndrome, which is a psychological pattern where you doubt your abilities and have a persistent fear of being exposed as a fraud. What's fascinating is how this mindset actually makes you more fragile and vulnerable to setbacks.

In this chapter, we'll explore how imposter syndrome and self-sabotage can act as internal barriers, preventing us from reaching our full potential, even after we've addressed our surface-level limiting beliefs. We'll also dive into how these psychological barriers can affect our relationship with money and success. Most importantly, we'll examine how transforming these barriers can be a crucial step toward becoming truly Antifragile - not just resistant to challenges, but actually strengthened by them. By the end of this chapter, you'll have strategies to overcome these internal obstacles and develop a healthier relationship with success and money.

Before we dive deeper, let me share a framework that will help you understand everything that follows. Here's a powerful analogy that changed my own life: our level of "success " in life is directly connected to our internal thermostat regarding our self-worth or worthiness. If you are sitting in a room right now and it is comfortable, chances are it is because of the thermostat. If it gets too cold, the heat comes on. If it gets too hot, the A/C comes on. This is also how our self-worth is regulated.

This self-worth thermostat is perhaps the single most powerful force determining your outcomes in life. It is all tied to our identity. If good things start to happen in our life—money, relationships, influence—and we don't think we are worthy, we will start to behave in ways that bring the temperature back down to where it is comfortable again. This is why lottery winners go broke and why dieters regain weight; their internal thermostat hasn't been reset.

WHO IS THAT IMPOSTER?

Let's start with imposter syndrome. By definition, imposter syndrome is the persistent inability to believe one's success is deserved or has been legitimately achieved as a result of effort and skills. People afflicted by imposter syndrome are afraid others are going to figure out they are a fraud and not deserving of the benefits received from all of their hard work. When I first encountered this concept, it seemed absurd, until I recognized it in myself and virtually every successful person I've met.

So how does this apply to us? First, breathe a sigh of relief. This is a universal human experience that affects both the extraordinarily successful and the everyday person alike.

Even though I fully understood this concept, I still struggled with this internal dialogue. "I know I have dreams and aspirations that are for the greater good. I understand that I need to feel, emotionally, as though I've *already* achieved my goals. But I also know I can't just sit on the couch and wait for things to appear in my life." How could I reconcile believing it has already happened with the reality that I still needed to do the work? The key lies in the word "I."

It took me a long time to realize that being overly focused on "I" was an ego-driven perspective. I needed to become crystal clear on WHAT I wanted, and yes, I had to do the work, but not from a place of ego. The breakthrough came when I finally understood that "I" was just a conduit for God (or the universe, source) to work through me and express himself through me. I realized that I was actually not that smart and not that strategic. I was getting help all along the way and didn't even recognize it. This shift in mindset brought me a sense of certainty and, even more importantly, peace. From then on, everything began to fall into place naturally, as I let go of control and trusted the process."

Looking back, I was so blessed to have been guided so eloquently, without even knowing it. Some would call it surrender. I now know and understand fully that highly "successful" people *never* accomplish great things by themselves. We all need help if we are going to live up to our full potential.

If the previous 2 paragraphs are not crystal clear in your mind, I suggest you re-read them until it sinks in. After all, it took me years to learn and apply this. Understanding this and taking action is key.

DON'T SABOTAGE YOUR IMPROVEMENT

Now, let's talk about self-sabotage. By definition, it means the act of behaving in a way that directly interferes with one's own goals, well-being, and relationships. Self-sabotage is an expression of lack of self-love. For example, you know you shouldn't drink another glass of whiskey, but hey, you "deserve" it, and it makes you feel good (until it doesn't) You may want a healthy body and mind, but you would rather be happy *now*. You know the right thing to do down deep, but that will have to wait till tomorrow. Then tomorrow it will have to wait until the next day, and there you go down the path. When you do things like this, you will never be truly happy or feel fulfilled.

How else could this play out in real life? Let's use weight loss as an example. Let's say you have a goal to lose 40 pounds. Things are going along wonderfully until you get to that last 10 pounds you want to lose. You find yourself eating things you know you shouldn't and skipping a workout here and there. You ask yourself, "What is going on here? I was so close!"

What many of us begin to do unconsciously is that even though we had the goal in mind, we begin to think about the consequences when we reach it. For instance: Will other people in our life be jealous of us and not want to hang with us anymore? Will people think that now we think we are better than them? Will some of our relationships change now that we can and want to do other activities that we couldn't do before? Maybe we lose a bunch of weight, and people begin to say things like, "Wow, you are getting skinny. Are you feeling okay?" If, down deep, we worry about these things, then we will start to behave in a way that sets us back to who we were before, and then we don't have to confront these perceived issues.

Here's another example of self-sabotage. You decide that this year is going to be different, so you create an elaborate vision board so you can see the things that you want to show up in your life every day. The problem is, if what you see on your vision board does not line up with your identity or belief system about who you are or can be, unfortunately, none of this will ever happen.

What will happen is your unconscious mind will say, "Oh, isn't that cute? Here he is again thinking all of those wonderful things. but we know if we just give it a couple of weeks, he will fall flat on his face as he has done before because he doesn't *really* believe in his heart of hearts that he can have those things or be those things." Has this kind of setback ever happened to you, despite your best intentions?

Maybe you can relate to this situation. Have you ever been around someone who always seems to have some medical problem? (We all know someone like this.) I want you to begin to pay close attention to these people. Some of them truly are sick and need and deserve our utmost empathy, but there are some who, down deep, do not want to get better. Some of them are not even aware they are behaving this way. Often, these people are just lonely and love the attention. If they are not "sick," then nobody comes around, and nobody brings them dinner or calls them to visit. A pattern begins to emerge that says, sick = attention, not sick = no attention. Therefore, it is no wonder they are always sick. They are self-sabotaging themselves to get attention. We need to recognize this and either help them find more ways to be valuable to others or show them healthier ways to get attention. I even heard a story of an older guy who shared that he was not feeling well. When asked how long he had been sick, he said, "In 3 weeks, it will be a month."

These patterns of self-sabotage don't happen in isolation; they're often reinforced by our social circles. If you find yourself falling just short of your goals all of the time, you may want to re-evaluate your decisions and relationships. Realize that most of the time your friends and family do not want you to change because they are afraid that if you change, you may no longer want to be their friend. It is way easier for them to bring you back down to where you used to be than for them to step up and become better themselves. If *you* get better, then, comparatively, they look worse. I am not saying who is right here or judging anyone. I just want you to realize that this commonly happens and you need to be aware of it. Make decisions that are right for you and the life you want and deserve to live.

WHAT DO YOU BELIEVE ABOUT MONEY?

Your beliefs about money operate largely below your awareness, in what psychologists call your unconscious mind. Understanding how this part of you works is crucial.

Some beliefs about money are harmful. Some of us were taught that there is only so much to go around, so you better protect yours or get your share, even at the expense of others. This scarcity mindset is the foundation of financial anxiety. Others might believe that money is evil, so you only need enough to get by, and rich people are greedy. Maybe someone taught you that wealthy people don't care about anyone else or they think they are better than others. While some of those things can be true, that is not the way it is for most people.

All of these are examples of beliefs. They have been pre-programmed in you from birth to age seven, and we make decisions based upon our beliefs. I like to describe this as a belief window. Let's say two of us are standing looking out a window at the same beautiful scene outside. If someone pulled us away, put us in two separate rooms, and asked us what we saw out the window, it would likely be two very different stories based upon our beliefs. Some people would focus on the beautiful colors and shapes of the trees, while others would focus on the piece of garbage that was left under the fence. Some would focus on the sky, and on and on. It was the same view, but people have completely different interpretations of what they saw. This is exactly how our unconscious mind works, and what we "see" is interpreted and defined through our beliefs.

This matters because we need to recognize that not everyone sees the same things that we see in life. This can be applied in real life to almost all situations. Heaven forbid, but let's talk politics for a moment. Let's say you have a particular political belief. Undoubtedly, you can find others with your same belief, regardless of whether it is actually factual or not. There is a fancy term for this called confirmation bias. Have you ever tried to get someone to change their belief or explain to them why they are wrong and you are right? The reason people don't budge is because you're trying to fix an unconscious belief (the preprogrammed beliefs) using conscious logic. You cannot change someone's unconscious beliefs by using conscious, logical thinking.

It's super important to understand this when you're trying to make your life more fulfilling, and hence be more Antifragile in the future. You need to identify these beliefs and contemplate whether or not they are serving you and in your best interest. Some people will call these limiting beliefs but by definition *any* belief has the potential to limit you from being your best self.

Let's apply this understanding specifically to money. Some of you feel like you don't deserve money or have had bad thoughts around money that you really need to get rid of. The best way I have found is to envision a little baby. For example, let's say it is your grandson or your granddaughter as a baby. There's absolutely nothing they don't deserve or that you wouldn't do for them, yet they really have done nothing to deserve that kind of love and abundance. Regardless of the fact that they have not contributed anything yet, they are still entitled to love and grace and protection. Well, newsflash: *so are you*. You are that same baby. You simply have a few more bumps and bruises from this thing called life. You are worthy of money and abundance in everything as well.

Money itself is not evil. What some people *do* with their money can be evil, but most people with an abundance of money use it for good. They use it to create more freedom for themselves, their families, and other causes that they care about. In my experience, people who have earned their money through hard work are some of the most generous people on the planet. The same does not apply to those who were given great wealth instead of earning it.

One of my mentors, Jim Rohn, put it this way: you don't earn a million dollars to earn a million dollars. You earn it to become the type of person who can make a million dollars. There's a big difference between the two. This is also the reason why most big lottery winners are often broke and unhappy within 10 years. They haven't learned the skills to handle that much energy because, after all, money is simply an exchange of energy.

When I receive it, I like to think of money as thank-you notes. In other words, people are saying thank you for the value or service I provided. This way, you can be more valuable to society as a whole, and if you ever lose that money, you have the skill set to do it over again. Remember that money in and of itself is not evil; it is what you do with the money that determines the value. For me, money equals freedom of choice and more ability to help others. Zig Ziglar said it best with, "Money isn't everything, but it ranks right up there with oxygen!"

THE POWER OF YOUR UNCONSCIOUS MIND

Now, let's talk about how our unconscious mind affects our relationship with money and success. What if I ask you to promise me that, whatever you do, you will *not* think about a big, beautiful, strong, powerful white horse? What did you immediately do? Yes, you saw a picture of a big, beautiful, strong, powerful white horse. Because I attached emotion to it with words like big, beautiful, strong, and powerful, it made it even more vivid in your mind. This is how your unconscious mind works, whether you know it or not.

Your unconscious mind cannot discern good, bad, right, or wrong. Those are things our conscious(thinking) mind attaches to words, usually based on previous experience. All the unconscious mind knows is what you thought of. You told it of a big beautiful, strong, powerful white horse, so that's what your unconscious mind heard, and that's what it will try to get more of for you in your life. You get more of what you focus on; it's as simple as that. Add thoughts attached to strong emotions or feelings to the mix, and it will put your unconscious mind into overdrive, trying to make the things you are focusing on a reality for you. Simply put, thoughts become things.

So I ask you: Are you focusing on a lack of anything like money, time, or relationships? Or, are you focusing on abundance of everything like money, relationships, opportunities, and possibilities?

KEEP YOUR WORD

Now let's explore another essential aspect of Antifragility: integrity. Be a man of your word and always do what you said you would do. This is essential to Antifragility. You have learned over the years that *not* being the kind of man who follows through with things is detrimental to others but, more importantly, harmful to your unconscious mind.

When you fail to follow through on commitments, you're not just letting others down—you're programming your unconscious mind to distrust yourself. Conversely, when you consistently honor your word, you build an unshakeable foundation of self-trust.

Being the kind of person who consistently does what you said you would do—someone who follows through on promises—builds integrity and trust. It also has a profound impact on every aspect of your life. Integrity is crucial for several reasons.

1. Builds Trust and Credibility

When you honor your commitments, whether they're personal or professional, you build trust with those around you. People will view you as dependable and reliable, and this reputation can open doors in your career, deepen relationships, and expand opportunities that you never dreamed possible. Credibility is the foundation for both personal and business success, and consistently doing what you said you would strengthens this foundation.

What's the impact? Trust leads to stronger, more meaningful relationships and professional opportunities because people are drawn to those they can rely on. People can energetically feel your integrity. This reliability often leads to leadership roles since people naturally follow those who demonstrate consistency.

2. Develops Self-Respect and Confidence

Following through on your word isn't just about earning the trust of others—it's about reinforcing your own self-worth. Every time you honor a commitment, you reinforce your belief in your own abilities. This consistency builds internal confidence, and over time, it creates a positive feedback loop where you trust yourself to achieve even bigger goals.

What's the impact? Increased self-confidence empowers you to take on new challenges. This upward spiral of self-assurance encourages you to set bigger, more meaningful goals in life. People with high self-respect are more Antifragile when facing adversity.

3. Strengthens Discipline and Accountability

Doing what you said you would do requires discipline and accountability. This self-discipline translates into all areas of life. It helps you establish good habits, meet deadlines, and avoid procrastination. The more you commit to tasks, the easier it becomes to discipline yourself to see them through, even when motivation wanes. This is why I tell my clients just beginning a new training plan to simply lace up their shoes, go outside, walk to the mailbox, and call it a win. Do the same thing tomorrow, but walk around the block. Start small and incrementally improve, but whatever you decide to do, just do it.

What's the impact? A disciplined, accountable mindset positively affects your health, finances, relationships, and career—*everything* leading to overall life improvement. For instance, sticking to a fitness routine or business goal becomes more manageable when you consistently practice self-discipline.

4. Fosters Better Decision-Making

When you make it a habit to follow through on promises, you become more mindful of the commitments you make. You say "no" to things that don't align with your values or priorities, or you know you are not going to do it. This practice leads to better decision-making and time management, as you focus only on what matters most.

What's the impact? You'll make fewer unnecessary commitments, avoid burnout, and gain a clearer sense of purpose in your actions. This leads to a more focused and intentional life, allowing you to direct your energy toward the things that truly move the needle.

5. Increases Influence, Leadership, and Well-Being

People who do what they said they would do inspire others. Whether it's in a personal relationship or a business setting, following through makes you a role model. When others see you leading by example, they are more likely to trust, respect, and follow your guidance. Leaders who consistently deliver are seen as credible and are naturally positioned to lead teams, communities, or even movements.

What's the impact? Strong leadership born from consistency creates more influence in social, professional, and community circles. This can lead to greater impact and the ability to inspire positive change in others.

By being the kind of person who does what you say you will do, you improve the quality of your relationships, build self-confidence, practice discipline, and become more intentional with your commitments. Building a habit of integrity not only leads to greater personal and professional success but also makes you a source of inspiration for those around you. People will literally feel your energy and want to be around you.

ANTIFRAGILE TACTICS

- Recognize Imposter syndrome is real and common, even among highly successful people

- Self-sabotage often stems from a lack of self-love and fear of change

- Your money mindset is shaped by early childhood experiences and beliefs

- Money itself is not evil; it's how it's used that matters

- Your unconscious mind doesn't distinguish between positive and negative thoughts; it simply tries to manifest what you focus on

- Focus on abundance rather than lack in all areas of your life

- Treat money as a "thank you" for the value you provide

- Develop the skills and mindset of a wealthy person, rather than just chasing the money itself

- Be the kind of person who does what you said you would do, without exception (be a man of your word)

- Remember that every time you say "I" did something, you didn't do it on your own. We all receive guidance if we just understand it, recognize it, and appreciate it

Now that we've explored the internal barriers of imposter syndrome, self-sabotage, and limiting money beliefs, we're ready to put this knowledge into action. In the next chapter, we'll discuss practical strategies for setting and achieving goals that align with your newfound Antifragile mindset and abundance-focused outlook. Remember, it's not just about knowing these concepts, but applying them consistently in your daily life to create lasting change.

CHAPTER 6

SETTING PROPER EXPECTATIONS FOR THE FUTURE

Do you suffer from Gerascophobia? Yes, gerascophobia, it is a fancy word that I had to look up to be sure I spelled it correctly, so as not to cause my editor to blow a gasket. Gerascophobia is essentially the fear of getting old. Now, I welcome getting old because I know that getting old is not the same as getting *older*, and I absolutely want to get older. Last I checked, there was only one way to not get older, and I want no part of that option for a long, long time.

When did we decide that the final third of our lives should be called "retirement"—as if we're somehow being put out to pasture? The very word suggests withdrawal, stepping back, fading away. Bullshit. I'm not retiring from anything. I'm *rewiring* myself for what could be the most meaningful and fulfilling phase of life. And if you're holding this book, I suspect you feel the same way.

This chapter is about setting proper expectations for your future, especially as you approach the back 9 of life. By understanding and preparing for what lies ahead, you can become Antifragile in the face of aging and turn potential challenges into opportunities for growth and fulfillment. It may be good to consider "retiring" toward something new and not away from something familiar but not fulfilling.

We'll explore how to shed society's outdated notions about aging, create a solid plan that excites rather than terrifies you, and take practical steps to ensure a vibrant and purposeful life as you age. For the record, I hate the word "retirement," so I am officially (hey, it's my story here) renaming it *rewirement*. This isn't about slowing down—it's about leveraging decades of hard-earned wisdom to create something even better.

DON'T FORGET: YOU WILL DIE SOMEDAY

The ancient Stoics had a great way of looking at our inevitable reality. They call it Memento Mori. Memento Mori literally means, "Remember, you must die!" It may sound morbid, but it was meant to have a positive connotation. It has the profound potential to wake us up and breathe more life into our lives. With this in mind, why in the world would we waste our precious little time here on earth worrying about something we have little control over? I have learned over the years that the things we worry about almost never actually come true, and the truly unfortunate things that sneak up and smack us in the side of the head are those things we didn't even see coming. With this in mind, let's move on and work on controlling the controllables and ignoring the things we cannot control.

Oftentimes, anxiety shows up when our perception of how the future will look and how it *actually* looks don't match. This is why social media is so dangerous, because sometimes it fools us into thinking we want a certain way of life. When we actually get there, however, we realize it's not all it's cracked up to be. The same applies to retirement. We've been sold images of silver-haired couples walking hand-in-hand on empty beaches, playing endless rounds of golf, or entertaining the grandkids in spotless homes. But real life doesn't work that way. Some days, your back hurts too much for golf. Some days, the grandkids are little terrors. Some days, you miss the sense of purpose your career gave you. The key is understanding that perfection isn't the goal—meaning is. And meaning comes from having realistic expectations while still maintaining hope.

Human beings have an innate need for hope for the future that is hardwired to move us forward. Hope for a better life, better relationships, and a more fulfilled life. This lack of hope is why we have so many problems with young poor people. They have difficulty envisioning a better future. Imagine what some of these people living in war zones today think. Some of them have lived with war, destruction, and lack of hope for years and honestly believe there is no end in sight. Others have hope that they will "win" the war and live happily ever after. Which group will continue to have the desire to keep up the fight? The group with hope for a better future. So, how can we utilize this observation to help us move forward?

The biggest reason older men are stressed about anything, especially retirement, is that they don't have the expectation or hope of a better life in retirement, and they don't have a plan. They have an idea of what it might look like, but that is a dangerous approach. For example, it's not a good way to enter into the retirement phase of your life with just an "idea." You better have a plan in place years ahead of time.

When you have a clear vision or path in mind, it becomes easier, more predictable, and more enjoyable. Any time spent on formulating a plan—any kind of plan—will put you light years ahead of most people. This alone will mitigate about 90 percent of the stress you feel. I also advise you to seek out coaches and planners who have done this for others successfully and follow their lead. In my experience, any money I have ever spent on coaching has always had at least a 2X return and oftentimes way more than that. When it comes to financial planning, do it often and start early. Compound interest may possibly be the eighth Wonder of the World.

DON'T SPEND A LOT OF TIME ON THAT

So what can we really expect later in life as a well-adjusted, dapper senior citizen? Well, some of the stuff is a little weird, and some is actually pretty cool. In the pretty weird category, we would have things like, why does the hair that previously adorned the top of our head decide to change residence to our ears? Where did my eyesight go? I used to be able to tie a #32 size fly on my line without magnification! Why does our skin begin to look like a fish we left a little too long out of the water? Why do we suffer from "bedroom disease," where things begin to move from our chest to our drawers? Why do our teeth begin to look the color of an old Mountain Goat? Well, I submit these things can be a bit surprising, and sometimes pretty damn comical, but I wouldn't spend a lot of time thinking about this. Control the controllables and move on.

Let's look at a great way to approach this whole business of setting the correct expectations and the power you take back by conducting yourself in such a way. You need to be careful not to let your ego get in the way when you decide to do something new. Has anyone ever told you that you need to get out of your own way? I had well-meaning people say that to me, but I always wondered what the hell that means. I didn't understand because I wasn't ready to understand it yet. I hadn't done what I now know as the "deep work." I didn't have the understanding of how the world (energy) really works.

There is the old saying, "When the student is ready, then the teacher will appear." This is important to understand. If you think *you* are in control of everything and *you* have to do everything yourself, then you are not ready to learn life's greatest, most mystical, and amazing lessons.

Most men I know spent decades in the trenches of hard work, grinding it out day after day. We were taught that's how you succeed. And it works…to a point. But as you approach this next phase, you need a different mindset. It's less about the constant grind and more about clarity of vision. What do you *actually* want this next chapter to look like? Not what your golf buddies want, not what the retirement brochures show, but what would make *you* feel alive and purposeful? Once you have that clarity, the path tends to reveal itself in ways you couldn't have planned.

Just start where you are at, rather than focus on any perceived limitations. For example, instead of feeling embarrassed about going to the gym or beginning a wellness program because you have let yourself go, forget about the past, *decide* you are going to go for it, and just begin. The only embarrassment that will come is if you don't do what your heart desires and you reach the end of life here on earth with regret. As Dr. Wayne Dyer wisely advised, "Don't die with your music still in you!" When you leave this earth, you cannot take what you have, but you can take what you gave!

We have all of these doubts and limiting beliefs, which we have discussed in detail. I encourage you to forget about the past "you." Give the past your heartfelt thanks for getting you this far, but it is time to say, "Thanks, I've got it from here." It is time to embrace and envision the present and future you.

CHANGE YOUR OIL

I would be remiss if I didn't discuss getting yearly physical exams done—or at least the most routine of them. Most of you guys take better care of your super-duty pickup trucks than you do your own bodies. Sure, you *can* drive it 50,000 miles and never change the oil, but just because you *can* doesn't mean you *should*. There could be some major breakdowns coming, right? Not getting annual exams is like trying to run a business but never keeping any books or being aware of the "numbers." Nobody would even think about doing that, but men frequently avoid looking at our own numbers. Here are some recommendations:

- Get a colonoscopy if you are at average risk by age 50, and sooner if you have a family history of polyps, colorectal cancer, or any other inflammatory bowel disease

- Get an annual dermatology assessment; catching things early is key

- See your Dentist annually

- Know your blood pressure and manage that if necessary

- Get annual comprehensive blood work, especially a hormone panel. You need to know those numbers

- And, for God's sake, get your annual prostate exam, especially if you have a family history of prostate problems

You'd rather wrestle a grizzly than get a prostate exam. But that little walnut-sized gland can cause a world of hurt if you ignore it. Catching problems early can mean the difference between a quick fix and a world of hurt. Sure, it can be unpleasant, but just get it done.

Put your exam appointments on your calendar, like all of your other important things that need to be done. When you are done with each exam, schedule the next year before you leave the office. Make it easy on yourself, and your wife (or whoever) shouldn't have to harp at you to get this done. You owe it to yourself and the people who care about you. I've known too many good men, including my own father, who've had to battle prostate cancer. It's a hell of a lot easier to deal with if you catch it early. And let's face it, a few seconds of discomfort is a small price to pay for peace of mind.

These check-ups aren't just about catching the bad stuff; they're also about optimizing your health. Your testosterone might be a bit low, or your vitamin D might be in the toilet. These are things you can fix and things that can make you feel like a million bucks if you address them. But you gotta know about 'em first. Don't die just because you ignored this stuff. Sadly, many men do.

ANTIFRAGILE TACTICS

- Embrace aging as a natural process and focus on getting older, not just getting old.

- Develop a positive mindset about the future by focusing on what you can control.

- Create a clear plan for retirement. Think about what excites you and what concerns you.

- Don't let your ego get in the way of personal growth and new experiences

- Take care of your health by getting regular check-ups and preventive screenings.

- Focus on the present and future you, rather than dwelling on past limitations. You can create a whole new identity TODAY.

- Remember that what you give in life is more important than what you have.

Now that we've set proper expectations for the future and learned how to approach aging with a positive mindset, let's dive into how you can put these ideas into action and create a fulfilling retirement lifestyle that keeps you vibrant, engaged, and Antifragile.

PART 3

BUILDING THE ANTI-FRAGILE BODY

CHAPTER 7

A HISTORY OF PHYSICAL FITNESS

It's 1972, and I'm a scrawny 12-year-old staring down a shiny new beast in the school gym. It looked part jungle gym, part medieval torture device, and somehow, it was supposed to make me strong. Enter the universal gym, the so-called "future of fitness." Little did I know this clunky metal contraption was just the beginning for me. Over the years, I've seen the world of health and wellness evolve in ways that would make even Jack LaLanne's head spin. From the sweatbands and shorty shorts of the '80s to today's obsession with kettlebells and CrossFit, we've all been on one hell of a ride. So buckle up—because the history of fitness is filled with as many fads and flops as breakthroughs. And trust me, some of it is as jiggly as that old belt machine that promised to melt the pounds off your waistline.

Looking back at the evolution of fitness isn't just an exercise in nostalgia—it's a way to separate timeless wisdom from marketing noise. As someone who's lived through fifty years of fitness revolutions and regressions, I can tell you: what's "revolutionary" is rarely new, and what's truly effective is rarely revolutionary.

This chapter isn't just a trip down memory lane. It's about understanding where we've been so we can figure out what really works. If you want to be Antifragile—the kind of man who gets stronger with every hit—you need to know the difference between fitness fads and true principles that stand the test of time. From Jack LaLanne fighting medical skepticism to the birth of gym culture to today's extreme ultramarathons, what we'll explore isn't just how equipment and methods changed but how our fundamental relationship with our bodies has evolved—and what that means for building your antifragile physique. Let's examine how we got here, where we went wrong, and what timeless principles remain standing.

THE "EASY" FITNESS SOLUTIONS

Let's start with that old universal gym. It was the first of its kind, designed to make fitness accessible by packing every exercise into one machine. You'd move from station to station, working different muscle groups, and supposedly come out stronger. Back then, we thought it was cutting-edge, even though it looked like a medieval rack meant for stretching us out more than building us up. The alternative? Giving free weights to a bunch of sugar-laden, ADHD afflicted 12-year-olds. Talk about a recipe for disaster. What could possibly go wrong, right?

Jack LaLanne was a legend, even if those workout coveralls were questionable. He was all about juicing (vegetables that is, not that kind of juicing we think of today) and staying fit way before anyone knew what that even meant. Jack was promoting fitness and lifting weights way before mainstream media figured it out.

What's often forgotten is how radical LaLanne's ideas were in his time. When he opened his first gym in 1936, doctors actively warned people against weightlifting, claiming it would make them "muscle-bound," cause heart attacks, and even diminish their sex drive. In an era when "healthy food" didn't exist and exercise was considered unnecessary for adults, LaLanne wasn't just ahead of his time—he was creating a new paradigm entirely. One story about him, in particular, I find quite amusing.

There was a local football team (I believe it was USC) practicing football near the beach one day. Jack was "working out" on the sandy beach when the coach asked him, "What are you doing?" Jack responded that he was lifting weights to get stronger and that the coach should consider incorporating that into the program.

At that point, the coach (a smartass) said, "Well, if you are so strong, then show me." Jack reportedly went up to the biggest guy on the team, threw him over his shoulders like a sack of potatoes, and ran up and down a sandy hill on the beach with this huge lineman on his back. (Jack was 5'6" and a buck fifty on the scale!)

The coach became convinced there was something to his method. That said, Jack was chastised by the medical community for telling people they should "work out." Doctors publicly called him a charlatan and a nutcase! They told Jack that working out with weights would cause people to have heart attacks and would lose their sex drive.

Jack defied those so-called "experts," lead by example, and proved them all wrong. Interestingly, he actually disliked lifting weights, but he knew if he did, and ate correctly, he would be hard to take down. Check out these other impressive stories about Jack:

- At age 42, he did 1,000 push-ups in 23 minutes. If you have ever done push-ups to failure once and then rested for a bit and tried to do some more—especially like, say, 900 more—*ouch*!

- At age 60, he swam from Alcatraz to Fisherman's Wharf wearing handcuffs and towing a 1,000-pound boat.

- To celebrate his 70th birthday, he swam a mile and a half along the California coast from Queensway Bridge to Long Beach harbor, all while wearing handcuffs and shackles on his legs and arms and towing 70 rowboats holding 70 people.

Jack lived to the ripe old age of 96 and likely would have lived longer except for the pneumonia that claimed his life.

In contrast, there was a "European Health Spa" in the town I grew up in. It was quite the opposite, but people there were still trying to do their very best, with the information they had, to take care of their bodies. One contraption of particularly amusing interest was this thing that looked like a treadmill platform, but rather than walking or running on it, you would stand there with this six-inch-wide "belt-like" thing around your backside, and it would jiggle the hell out of you. All the jiggling had the specific duty of "burning" fat off of the midsection. To this day a scar still exists in my young soul reliving the vision of those "plesantly plump" ladies getting jiggled. You just can't unsee that.

Then in the 1980s, more machines began to come onto the scene. Before this, weight-lifting was done predominantly with free weights like barbells and dumbbells. Actually, I have always wondered who thought of calling them dumbbells, and who wanted to actually lift dumbbells?

Maybe it's just me, but why not smartbells or something else? Anything but dumbbells! Anyhow, weight-lifting was beginning to be more in vogue so the masses were flocking to it. The problem was, training large numbers of people at once (think sports teams), required a lot of equipment and space.

As weight training gained mainstream popularity, gyms faced a new problem: how to train large groups efficiently and safely. The solution? Machines that isolated specific muscles and guided your movement patterns. The Nautilus revolution was born.

Thus, machines that worked specific parts of the body, like "Nautilus," grew in popularity. Then, the marketeers began to show up with their version of a "better" mousetrap.

This shift represents a critical turning point in fitness history: we began prioritizing convenience and safety over effectiveness.

While machines made gyms more accessible and less intimidating, they also disconnected us from the integrated, full-body movements that built Jack LaLanne's functional strength. About that same time, a guy (at least I think he was a guy) named Richard Simmons came along. The ladies loved him. But guys, not so much. He was one of the first people promoting "aerobic" exercise.

Most people had no clue that aerobics was an actual medical term. By definition, aerobics is "relating to, involving, or requiring free oxygen," or "denoting exercise that is intended to improve the efficiency of the body's cardiovascular system to absorb and transport oxygen."

This new concept led to the beginning of group classes, which was of particular interest at the time, especially for the ladies. For macho guys like me it was "no bueno" because I did *not* want to be in any way affiliated with Richard. Despite my apprehension, the concept was here to stay.

I must say, a version of Richard's aerobics is still a big part of my regimen, minus the headband and the shorty shorts. Nobody wants to see that on me, take my word for it.

Group fitness in a specific facility began to be a major social shift. It became a place for social interaction, camaraderie, and accountability to others with our fitness (like, "Where the hell is Joe today? He is supposed to spot me").

This shift brought something crucial that was missing from the isolated, machine-based approach: community. For the first time, fitness became both social and accessible to average people. But this accessibility came with a dark side that would eventually emerge.

MORE IS NOT ALWAYS BETTER

The word was getting out about the value of lifting heavy things and moving, but here came the marketers once again. Bigger, better gyms with more and more amenities began to spring up. Misinformation, or maybe I should say overly-embellished information, began to appear on the scene.

Some of it was great and helped further our understanding of the principles, but some of it was marketing hogwash and it continues as such to this day.

If a little is good, then more is better, right? Not so fast there. Once people started being more intentional with their fitness, some would start to see results, but eventually, they would often reach a plateau when it came to their progress. Consequently, they decided they had to do more and more.

For example, let's look at the sport of running. It began as walking with some occasional running (you know, to go run down the gazelle). Then, it actually progressed to "jogging," which was faster than walking but not an all-out effort and for a fairly short duration, say 20-30 minutes.

Well then, if 30 minutes is good, then an hour would be amazing. And then, if we can "jog" for an hour, why not step it up to running for an hour? Enter the 10K race. It must be better right? Then a half—or God forbid a full—marathon, that must be *great* for you.

When marathons became ho-hum, well let's do a 50K and even 100K became the next goals. The problem with this way of thinking is that, while challenges can be good for you, there comes a point when it is too much, and your body breaks down from an overall health standpoint. That point is different for everyone.

Thank God people are now becoming more aware of the balancing act it takes to optimize your physicality, because it is different for everyone. We are beginning to see it more and more in the news. Healthy-looking people are beginning to tip over or begin to break down as a result of over-training or PESs (performance-enhancing substances).

So, what most of us are really searching for is the MED (minimal effective dose). In other words, what amount of training will get the biggest return on investment? Spoiler alert: It turns out the good news is that this is way less work than you would think. The key is doing the work over a long period of time.

The great news is you do *not* need (or want) to do any of these extreme behaviors. We will get into this later in the book.

Now, the problem becomes that there really are not a lot of ways to "market" the tried and true principles. Consequently, "new" things are coming out daily, with the latest and greatest as a way to get you to buy something. Some of that is all fine and well and there are good new products out there—but all I am saying is beware.

It is important to understand how physical fitness has evolved over time. This is in no way an exhaustive review of the history of training or wellness, but I think you get the point.

Yes, we do have some amazing new ways to train and build community, but the actual principles really have not changed over the last 75 years.

ANTIFRAGILE TACTICS

- The basic principles of training and nutrition for the most part have all been figured out by now

- If you start with the basics and do them a consistent basis over time, you will get the results you are looking for

- Follow Jack LaLanne's advice from years ago. Exercise is King, Nutrition is Queen, and if you have both you have a Kingdom

- Finally, not to get on my soapbox here, but I think it is important to learn from history but not be judgmental. Most people do the best they can with the information they had *at that point in time*! We tend to judge things from the past based upon our understanding *today*, and that is not fair, beneficial, or helpful to anyone. Let's be kind, tolerant, and forgiving toward one another

It doesn't do anybody any good to tear down statues from our past. 'Nuff said! Now, let's move on by discussing something you encounter multiple times per day: food and nutrition.

CHAPTER 8

NUTRITION SIMPLIFIED

As a dentist for three decades, I've seen more than my fair share of mouths. But it wasn't until I started paying attention to what was going into those mouths that I really began to understand whole body health. My journey from fixing teeth to fixing lives has been quite a ride, filled with hunting and fishing trips in my beloved Montana, bartending adventures in college, and a whole lot of nutritional experimentation. Now, as a wellness coach, I'm here to share what I've learned about the fuel that keeps our bodies running.

In this chapter, we're going to break down nutrition into simple, actionable principles that work for almost everyone. No fad diets, no complicated rules—just straightforward actionable advice that you can start using today to improve your health and vitality.

SIMPLIFYING NUTRITION PRINCIPLES

Talking about nutrition can be as contentious as discussing politics or religion. Everyone's got an opinion, and they're usually passionate about it. You can find "evidence" to support just about any diet out there. Paleo, Keto, Vegan, Pescatarian, Carnivore—you name it—someone's swearing by it.

But what if I told you that the best approach isn't about following a strict diet, but about understanding basic principles that work for most people? Wouldn't that be easier? That's what we're going to dive into.

I've spent decades observing what happens when people make specific nutritional changes, and the patterns are remarkably consistent. In my experience, a plant-forward approach with lots of lean protein sources is about as good as it gets for a one-size-fits-all approach. This means eating a huge variety of plants that are different colors daily, along with protein and fat. It's simple, it's flexible, and it works for most people.

 Both Oreos and opium can be considered vegan, but does that make them good for you? Of course not. Even though I am not and never have been vegan, I applaud people who are because it means that, at a very minimum, they are being intentional about what they are putting in their "pie hole."

Let's look at and define macronutrients. There are three: protein, fat, and carbohydrates. How you balance these three elements determines virtually every aspect of your nutritional health.

CONFUSING CARBOHYDRATES EXPLAINED

Now, let's talk about the macronutrient that seems to cause the most confusion: carbohydrates. Understand that even though carbohydrates are discussed as "essential" macronutrients, they really aren't. By definition, essential means that you must get them from your diet. But that isn't true. The body can synthesize these endogenously (on its own) and can also use alternative fuels for all bodily functions. That said, they are important from a vitamin and mineral standpoint.

Carbohydrates come in two primary forms: simple and complex. Simple carbs—like table sugar, fructose in fruit and honey, candy, and sugary drinks—are quickly broken down and spike blood sugar rapidly. Complex carbs—found in vegetables, legumes, and whole grains—are sugar molecules linked in long chains that require more time to digest, resulting in steadier energy and blood sugar levels.

The main reason complex carbs are better for you is because they more closely resemble their unadulterated "natural" state and still contain fiber, which slows the increase in blood sugar. Complex carbs are more likely to contain vitamins and minerals than their simple carb siblings.

Let's talk about bread because it is a favorite of most people and can be confusing, so it's worthy of special attention. We've all heard that whole grain breads are better in general. Here's a nasty little secret: not all breads are created equal. In fact, the processing method matters more than many realize. One study I loved was where they took the same grain and ground it in different ways. What they found every time was that the finer ground varieties always spiked the blood sugar higher, even if it was the exact same grain.

Most bleached white breads only contain the endosperm, stripping away most of the good stuff. Whole wheat bread is your best choice as the grain is mostly intact. Watch out for marketing tricks. "Wheat" bread doesn't necessarily mean whole wheat. And "multigrain" just means there's more than one type of grain, but it doesn't guarantee they're *whole* grains.

Then there's sourdough. Most store-bought brands of sourdough bread are not true sourdough. Here's the way to tell: Look at the label and unless the first ingredient says something like sourdough cultures or starters, it isn't real sourdough. Look for real sourdough because it offers advantages on how it impacts blood sugar.

One last caveat about bread. If you look in the freezer section, you can often find sprouted grain breads. These are breads made from grains that have been sprouted and then made into bread. Sprouted whole grain and true sourdough are my go-to choices. Be careful here. Bread is not for every meal, and I'm not saying to have three or four slices. Go easy and use bread as a treat, not a staple.

THE IMPORTANCE OF VEGETABLES

Now, let's talk about one of the most important parts of a healthy diet: vegetables. Here's a concept that has been around for years. Remember mom harping at you to "Eat your vegetables?" Because, she said, "There are starving kids in Africa!" While Mom's global awareness was commendable, there are other reasons to heed Mom's advice. Color means certain nutrients are present in the food. This means we should eat a huge variety of plants that are different colors daily.

When you eat vegetables, freshness drastically impacts both nutritional value and taste. As a child who raided neighborhood gardens, I discovered something most adults forget: fresh vegetables taste incredible on their own. That sweet corn eaten straight from the stalk or carrots pulled from the soil contained not just soil microbes that strengthened our immunity but also enzyme-rich nutrition still intact. The further we move from that garden-fresh state, the more nutritional value we lose.

We need a variety of micronutrients and minerals and vitamins for our bodies to work properly. What is the best way to easily incorporate this into your daily life? Be sure you have a colorful plate. The most colorful plate wins, every time! Color = vitamins and minerals, simple as that.

Here's a good way to look at this so that it becomes actionable. Strive for two servings a day of each color (a serving is essentially a half cup, so one cup a day of different colored veggies). For example:

- Red = tomatoes, red peppers, and strawberries

- Orange = sweet potato, carrots, and orange bell peppers

- Yellow = yellow bell peppers, squash, and corn

- Green = asparagus, celery, spinach, and broccoli

- Blue/Purple = blueberries, purple cabbage, and eggplant

- White/tan = cauliflower, mushrooms, onions, and garlic

This is simple and nutritious, and the associated fiber is a huge bonus. Everybody talks about probiotics these days, but prebiotics are equally important. Prebiotics are essentially the fiber that the probiotic bacteria feed on. Vegetables provide this critical prebiotic fiber that nourishes your gut bacteria, allowing them to produce short-chain fatty acids that regulate inflammation, mood, and even brain function. This fiber-bacteria relationship may be the most underappreciated aspect of nutrition today.

PROTEIN SOURCES AND HUNTING PHILOSOPHY

For protein sources, my go-to is wild game (venison, elk) and lean cuts of meat. While we're on the subject of hunting, I would ask that you keep an open mind. Hunting to me is something that is more than killing an animal; it is sacred to me. If done properly, it actually is one of the most humane ways for an animal to die in the wild.

This is obviously my opinion, and I respect your right to disagree, but I stand by my conviction that hunting, if done as a sacred act, is one of the purest human things we can do. "Hunting" to me is so much more than the actual killing of an animal. It involves planning, problem-solving, getting together with family and friends in the outdoors, and gathering amazing experiences and stories to share with future generations. It is the epitome of Antifragility.

Here's another thing to contemplate regarding eating meat. I hear a lot of people advocating that humans are not meant to eat meat. Well, as I have already said, I am a dentist by trade, so I am pretty much an expert regarding teeth. What I have noticed quite glaringly is that any animal that has canine teeth is meant or designed to eat meat. We have canines, as humans. We were designed to eat meat.

You may be curious about lean meat versus fatty cuts of meat. I favor lean cuts when possible because most of the toxins (if any) are found in the fat, not the lean part. I enjoy a good ribeye occasionally as well. The fat is delicious. But most of the time, stick to the pasture-raised and lean cuts of meat. And find a way to get fish into your regular diet.

When it comes to fish, we need to be careful with mercury content. I prefer wild-caught salmon, sardines, and anchovies. Larger predator fish (fish that primarily eat smaller fish) have higher mercury content because they have their own mercury burden plus that of the fish they eat as well (think swordfish here).

Tuna (a large predator fish) is not going to kill you if you eat it in moderation. Safe Catch does a mercury test on each batch of tuna.

Eggs are another great source of protein, and yes, eat the yolk too. Egg yolks contain choline which is something most of us need. When it comes to eggs, I prefer pasture-raised or free-range organic when possible. Be careful here, there are actually seven types of eggs available: vegetarian, free-run, free-range, omega 3, processed, vitamin enhanced, and organic. Don't get caught up in the marketing.

FATS AND THEIR ROLE IN DIET

The final macronutrient is fat. This is the dietary boogeyman that has been unfairly demonized for decades. Fat is the most calorically dense macronutrient coming in at nine calories per gram (compared to four for protein and four for carbs). There are do's and don'ts when it comes to fat. First off, we were all led down the wrong path during the low-fat craziness of the past.

Any data comparing the implementation of a low-fat diet and incidence of "all cause" disease appears conclusively to show that as soon as we started eating a low-fat diet, the disease rates went up, not down. Two obvious reasons exist for this outcome. First, the only way manufacturers could get us to eat these "fatless" products was to add lots of sugar to make them palatable. The second reason was because they failed to distinguish between "good" and "bad" fats.

Here's a quick breakdown of the types of fats:

- Monounsaturated fats: olive oil, avocados, almonds, and pumpkin seeds

- Polyunsaturated fats: sunflower and other seed oils, walnuts, and fish

- Saturated fats: chicken, beef, cheese, coconuts, and palm oil

- Trans fats (hydrogenated): vegetable oils, margarine, and shortening—the true dietary villains

Then, there are omega-3 and omega-6 fatty acids. Everything has a ratio of omega-3 to omega-6 fatty acids. The modern diet has thrown this ratio completely out of whack. It provides an overabundance of omega-6 foods (processed foods and seed oils) and not enough omega-3 (fish oil, salmon, oysters, sardines, flaxseed, chia seeds, and walnuts).

Here's my simple Antifragile Tactic to fats:

- Avoid seed oils like sunflower, safflower, canola, soybean, and corn. These are inflammatory time bombs

- Skip the French fries (high heat, seed oil, and high starch also create inflammation problems).) Substitute a salad

- Use high "smoke-point" oils to cook with (I use avocado oil). If the pan smokes, that's not great for your health

- Consume ample amounts of MCTs (medium chain triglycerides like coconut oil) for brain and metabolic health

- Use extra virgin olive oil ("Italian butter") liberally, especially when not cooking with it

- Be skeptical about "low-fat "foods; read the label to see what they added in place of the fat—usually, it's sugar

- Eat high omega-3 foods like fish oil, sardines, wild salmon, mackerel, nuts, and seeds like flax and chia

CALORIES, METABOLISM, AND MACRO TRACKING

Although our bodies are extremely complex, the basic premise of calories in calories out applies to the human body, but it's not really that simple. And please hear this: you *cannot* out-exercise poor nutrition! Just get that nonsense out of your head. Stop with the endless slogging on the treadmill to "burn calories." The way to be fit and lean is to burn more calories at rest or when you are sleeping by raising your basal metabolic rate (ie. build muscle, lose fat).

You must track your macros or macronutrients like protein, fat, and carbs. You do not necessarily need to do this for the rest of your life (although I do), but you do need to know how your body responds to different inputs and adjust accordingly. People say this is a pain in the ass, but so is a heart attack. There are many apps to help you with tracking. One example would be My Fitness

Pal. I can already hear some people complaining that tracking is time-consuming and you have to track everything you eat. My response is either take time now, or wait till the diseases show up and then you will have to make time, and it will be an uphill battle for sure.

It amazes me how people shove things into their mouth having no idea what is in that food, good and bad. This would be analogous to a company operating with no way to track metrics. Who in their right mind would invest in a company that had no way to track what was going on? Certainly not me. So why is it okay to treat the most amazing assets we have (our body and health) so haphazardly?

ALCOHOL AND ADDICTIVE SUBSTANCES

Let's address the nutritional elephant in the room, alcohol. Everyone preaches moderation, but alcohol's "slippery slope" is steeper than most realize.

I like my clients to consider how a person who never drank any alcohol would feel the next morning if they drank as much as they did yesterday. Do you think it is good for your overall health to get "used to" consuming this much alcohol? It truly is amazing to me how many "functioning alcoholics" are out there.

How do you know if you have a problem? If your drinking starts to have a negative effect on any of your interpersonal relationships, *you* have a drinking problem. It's a huge red flag, so beware.

I teach my clients who want to quit drinking alcohol to totally reframe what *not* drinking alcohol actually signals. When us old guys saw one of our older buddies riding a bike, we thought, "Oh look, Lenny must have gotten a DUI." Today, most people would think, "Oh, look, he is getting some exercise."

Re-frame your mindset around alcohol. Rather than thinking you're missing out on the party, think about taking care of yourself.

I predict that in the near future, all of the "cool kids" will not be drinking (much) alcohol. I already see more venues offering "mocktails" and NA beers. I have to say that 100 percent of my clients who do quit or cut way back on alcohol consumption always say it was one of the best things they did. Lastly, remember that younger people are watching what we do and look up to us. Be sure you are setting a good example.

The other addictive substance I must discuss is tobacco use, especially "chewing" tobacco. As a professional dentist, I have seen more dire consequences from long-term chewing tobacco than most people realize. Obviously, the first and most widely known problem with chewing tobacco is the potential for mouth cancer. The other universal problem is that it is very abrasive. I saw crazy erosion of gum tissue from chewing tobacco. Some people lost teeth because all of their gum tissue was gone. Again, when you were a kid and first "took a dip" (no, not in the pool), do you remember how you got dizzy and nearly puked? I sure do, and I certainly never wanted to get used to that.

INTERMITTENT FASTING AND CRAP FOODS

While there is a lot of hype these days about intermittent fasting, I think there are some important things to consider. First off, by intermittent fasting most people are really talking about a restricted feeding window. For example, no eating from 9:00 P.M. to 10:00 A.M or whatever fits your lifestyle. During that time, you are not eating, only consuming water, coffee, and some teas. The rest of the day you can eat "normally."

The reason it works, at least in the short term, for many people is because you are restricting overall "calories-in" most of the time. If you are in a caloric deficit (burning more than you take in), you will lose weight. This is universally true. But it's not that simple. For some people, it can place more stress on an already stressed system.

The trap I have seen clients fall into is they think that because they are restricting the time they are eating, it is "open season" for the rest of the day. Their mentality becomes, "Bring on the chocolate cake! No, not a piece, the whole cake dammit, because I deserve it!" The reality check is that attitude is dysfunctional and will not serve anyone well..

The bottom line here is try it if you are curious. Keep track of how you feel, how you are sleeping, your mental clarity, your energy levels, and your digestion. If it works for you, go for it.

Now let's talk about CRAP foods. This is an acronym for Calorie-Rich And Processed foods. Most of us know which foods are

CRAP and which ones are better choices. A great place to start is to avoid pasta, rice, potatoes, and refined flour. These foods alone are not villainous, but if you eat them in the quantities found in the SAD (Standard American Diet), they can be disastrous for long-term health.

Hunger is one concept that is not discussed enough. Be aware that there are different kinds of hunger. There is biological hunger brought on by a cascade of events that happen automatically at the cellular level. Two hormones in particular are key players here. Ghrelin is a hormone that signals the need to eat, and Leptin sends the signal to stop eating. As an aside, do you ever wonder why Grandma told you to slow down and chew your food? Well, maybe she knew that if you stuff yourself too quickly (think Thanksgiving), by the time the leptin signal comes in, you have already overeaten. Hey, has anybody seen Grandpa? Look on the couch.

Understanding the difference between emotional hunger and biological hunger is key to mastering nutrition. Biological hunger is our body's genuine need for nutrients, a signal that typically appears gradually and can be satisfied by almost any wholesome food. Emotional hunger, on the other hand, often emerges suddenly and urgently, driven not by physical need but by stress, boredom, or feelings of emptiness.

While biological hunger nourishes the body, emotional hunger seeks comfort, often leading us to reach for foods high in sugar, fat, and salt. By tuning in to these signals, we better understand our true needs, aligning our eating habits with what strengthens our bodies and supports our long-term vitality.

Use the "apple test" to tell the difference between the type of hunger you might be experiencing. Before you eat something, ask yourself, "Would I eat an apple instead?" If the answer is no, then you might be eating it for reasons other than biological hunger.

Another thing to contemplate is the order in which you eat your foods. This can make a big difference in your health. Try eating your veggies first(carbs and fiber). Then, protein and fats. Lastly, (if at all) eat the starches (potatoes, pasta, etc). Always eat slowly and intentionally, not with your face glued to the television or phone. Be sure to chew food thoroughly as well. These "little things" aid your digestion and help extract the proper nutrients from your food.

While it is true that we need to incorporate most of the behaviors from this book into our daily routine, one can argue that some are more important than others. Nutrition or fueling your body, however, is a non-negotiable.. a zero sum game.

If you neglect proper nutrition, you will have a difficult time making progress. Remember learning multiplication in school? The rule is any number when multiplied by zero equals zero. So, while you may train on a regular basis, practice stress management techniques, get your mind right, and surround yourself with an amazing community, if you do not fuel your body properly, you are multiplying by zero. You can negate a lot of hard work by not eating in a healthful way.

ANTIFRAGILE TACTICS

Remember, nutrition doesn't have to be complicated. Here's my Antifragile strategy to wrap things up: (Pick the low hanging fruit, easy things first, and you will be 80 percent of the way there).

- Shop the perimeter of the store (pay attention to this, most of the CRAP is on the inner aisles).

- Have a colorful plate (try new veggies).

- When possible, eat veggies first, then protein and fat, and starches last

- Minimize the white guys (rice, pasta, refined flour, sugar, potatoes, etc). They are a treat, not a staple.

- Track and know the macros in your foods. Track your results for a year.

- Limit yourself to a maximum of two alcoholic drinks a day for guys (Look up how much volume is considered a drink) and one for women. (set boundaries)

- Be intentional when you eat. Have a plan, don't mindlessly shove whatever down your gullet). Veggies first, protein and fat second, and starches last(if at all)

- Maybe start by just eliminating ONE thing like soda pop or French fries, then add other things when that behavior is mastered.

- Pay attention to labels. For example, almost all "Protein bars" are just glorified candy bars.

- Pay attention to how certain foods make you feel. (Are you farting, belching, sleepy, etc.?)

- Eat foods in their natural state. (There should only be one ingredient on the ingredient legend.)

- Avoid cheap seed oils. (Instead, use ghee, grass-fed butter, extra-virgin olive oil, and/or avocado oil instead).

- Drink half your body weight in ounces of water every day. Consider adding a pinch of pink sea salt and a little lemon.

- Almost all of my adult clients are getting too many carbs, too much fat, and not enough protein when they start my program!

- Nutrition can be a zero-sum Game

- Almost everyone will need a protein supplement. Grass-fed, pasture-raised whey protein isolate is the gold standard. (A good rule of thumb is 1 gram per pound of *desired* body weight.)

- Remember the "apple test"—if you feel "hungry" but wouldn't want to eat an apple, then maybe it's not really hunger.

Now that we've covered the basics of fueling your body, let's discuss how to move that body effectively.

In the next chapter, we'll dive into the world of fitness and exercise, exploring how to build strength, improve endurance, and maintain flexibility as you age. Remember, a well-oiled machine needs good fuel and regular maintenance! Imagine what would happen if you wanted to perform like a jet airplane that needs jet fuel, but you only supply it with low octane unleaded gas. You would never get off the ground. Neither your body nor your life will take off if you don't fuel yourself properly. The body and mind are intricately connected, so you need to work on both. The exciting part is that when you make either one better, it automatically stimulates the other to grow. It's important to know that we have control. However, we have to *take* that control. I'll see you there.

CHAPTER 9

TRAINING AND RECOVERY SIMPLIFIED

Imagine a drug that could reverse aging, build strength, boost energy, improve mental clarity, and enhance your entire quality of life. This miracle exists—but it's not sold in bottles. It's the deliberate practice of training your body, and it's the cornerstone of becoming what I call an "Antifragile Human."

Most people avoid training not because it's truly difficult but because they've overcomplicated it. They've been sold on the idea that effective fitness requires specialized equipment, complicated routines, or superhuman willpower. They're wrong.

The point of this chapter is simple: effective training doesn't need to be complicated. We're going to cut through the noise of flashy fitness trends and overpriced programs to focus on the timeless, proven principles that actually work. By understanding and applying these fundamental concepts, you can transform your body, improve your health, and become what I call an "Antifragile Human," which is someone who grows stronger in the face of stress and adversity.

Forget about those infomercials that drone on trying to sell you something. The *principles* are simpler than anything you can buy on television, and they never change. The act of lifting weights (moving with some means of resistance) is a perfect example of being an Antifragile Human. Lifting weights stresses your body to the point that it must grow back stronger. This stress/adversity is the exact signal your body needs to initiate growth and hypertrophy of muscle. The body actually overcompensates for the stress placed on it by building back stronger. Antifragility at its finest hour!

Antifragile systems improve when exposed to the right kind of stress, unlike things that are merely robust (able to withstand stress) or resilient (able to recover from stress). Your body is the perfect example.

When you lift weights, you create controlled damage to your muscle fibers. Your body responds by not just repairing those fibers but building them back stronger than before. This adaptation mechanism is the essence of antifragility—and it's why proper training is so powerful. You're not just maintaining your body; you're programming it to continuously improve.

Now, let me share a few observations from my 50 years in the fitness world that will help you understand how to apply these simple principles effectively:

One of my most perplexing observations is what I call the ripped trainer, out-of-shape trainee phenomenon. I've watched many people hire a trainer and never see any body composition changes, sometimes after years of training with that individual. I applaud both the trainer and trainee for their effort and dedication, but often what works for the trainer doesn't work for the trainee, especially if there is a huge age discrepancy. If hiring a trainer, sit down ahead of time and really get on the same page about your expectations and what will be required to reach your goals.

Fitness is only about the journey, never the destination. The reason for this is that high achievers are always looking for the next step, the next level, the next gear. This is a good thing, because you can always get one percent better in anything.

The other elephant in the room here is nutrition. If you do not dial in your nutrition, getting the "look" you want will be very difficult if not impossible. Remember the old adage: Abs are made in the kitchen, not the gym!

JUST ONE MORE DAY

One of the biggest mistakes I see people make is they decide on January 1 that this year is going to be *the* year. They jump into working out with more enthusiasm than they've ever had. The next day, they can barely walk. With their new resolve, they hit it again, only this time they go so hard they injure themselves. Now, they *have* to rest. It wasn't that they didn't give it the old college try; they just had bad luck or bad genes, right? Then they go tell their friends how they tried but it wasn't their fault, and the cycle begins all over again next January 1. I have seen this over and over, nearly every year. I also always wonder, "What is so magical about January 1? If you are going to do this, then just start right now, today!"

I recommend that clients take a clue from the Alcoholics Anonymous playbook. Their rule is: "Just one more day." Don't go into this thinking you must work out and eat nutritiously for the rest of your life. That seems daunting for a lot of people. Instead, think, "I am going to eat nurturing foods and lift heavy things today, and then tomorrow, get up and decide to do it *one more day*." Before you know it, you'll have established a new behavioral pattern, and I can assure you, there will come a time where you wouldn't dream of treating your body badly. You will hate it if you miss a workout. In the beginning, just stack up the wins. Focus on the behavior, not the results.

Some of us have this bizarre all-or-nothing mentality. We figure if we're not punishing ourselves with Navy SEAL-level BUD/S training, why bother? This macho nonsense is the enemy of sustainable fitness. Instead, focus on *functional fitness*—training that enables you to do whatever you want in real life with ease and enjoyment.

I love being outdoors: playing with my grandkids, hunting, fishing, and being with my friends, family, and horses. It always amazes me how some of my friends who are not in the best shape can keep right up with me the first day. They can ride 20 miles or hike long trails often while carrying a pack, and they seem to love it. Afterwards, we get back to camp, start the fire, enjoy a little "happy hour," eat some amazing food, and embellish a story or two. The next morning, I began to notice that the wheels were starting to fall off for them. They are slow to get up and sometimes don't. They begin to make rumblings that maybe they will just stay in camp today and keep the fire warm.

This is what I mean by functional fitness. Everybody can do amazingly well—for a day. I want you to be able to do that day after day, week after week, and year after year. That is my goal for you because I promise life is better and so much more fulfilling this way. The reason most older men quit doing the things they love is because it *hurts*—and if you are in pain, it's hard to have a good time. However, do not conflate fitness with pain. The reason these men are in pain is because they do not train! I hear many men get it backwards; they think they cannot train because they are in pain. It doesn't work that way.

THE FUNDAMENTALS OF ANTIFRAGILE TRAINING

Your training approach should be built on three non-negotiable fundamentals:

1. Proper form always comes first. I see too many men at the gym swinging weights they can't control, sacrificing range of motion, and setting themselves up for injury. Your ego has no place in your workout. Use full range of motion (complete contraction and relaxation of the muscle) and weights you can actually control.

2. Progressive overload is the master key: Simply put, you must continually challenge your muscles with increasing demands over time. This doesn't always mean adding more weight—you can increase repetitions, slow down the movement, or decrease rest periods. The essential point is that your body adapts to exactly what you ask of it, no more and no less.

3. Consistency trumps perfection. In the beginning, focus on establishing the habit rather than optimizing every detail. Be "consistently inconsistent"—do something physical every day, but vary what you do to keep it interesting and incorporate different aspects of fitness.

DON'T BE THE "OLD MAN"

Another big mistake I see at the gym is that people dink around between sets, especially if they are retired and have all day. They do a set and then get on their phone for five minutes, watching some mind-numbing video or some other time drain. Be aware of your intensity. There was a saying in the bodybuilding days of yore that said "intensity for immensity." The benefit of intensity in your workouts is twofold: 1) the muscle fibers (both fast *and* slow twitch) will get way more stimulation and 2) you will get your heart rate rockin' to reap the benefit of a "cardio" workout.

Let's look at the stereotypical caricature of an "old man." Bent over and decrepit, right? Now, remember your head weighs about 11 pounds. And walking is just moving your legs forward as you lean forward so you don't fall flat on your face. So how do we help ourselves continue to walk upright with good posture?

It all starts with strength in what's called the posterior chain. This refers to all of the muscles from the back of your head to your butt, and even down the back of your leg. These are the often overlooked muscles that become weaker over time due to poor posture and being slumped over a desk for most of our life. Focus on muscles in the back of your body more than the muscles in the front of your body. Men are especially guilty of this because they tend to focus on the muscles they see in the mirror (think chest, biceps, and abs) and neglect the ones that keep them standing tall and proud.

To avoid becoming this caricature, you need to prioritize your posterior chain—the muscles running from the back of your head down to your heels.

Here's what happens when you neglect posterior chain training:

1. Your shoulders round forward

2. Your head juts forward (adding strain to your neck)

3. Your hips tilt, creating lower back pain

4. Your knees and ankles absorb excessive impact

Incorporate exercises that specifically target these areas. Deadlifts, rows, face pulls, and glute bridges should form the foundation of your training, not the afterthoughts.

As we get older, we need to place more emphasis on recovery from training as well—not just injury. Muscle takes time to build. The basic rule of recovery and muscle adaptation is simply do not train the exact same muscle group on consecutive days. Leave at least a day in between, and possibly two.

ANTIFRAGILE MEN FIND A WAY

Our bodies aren't meant to be preserved through avoidance. They're designed to adapt and grow stronger when properly stressed. You were meant to transform aging from a process of decline into an opportunity for unprecedented strength and vitality.

Let me address one other common misconception as we get older. You may say to me, "But Gene, you don't understand. I have an injury to yada yada yada or I have this condition or disease that prevents me from doing any of this stuff." Now, I'm not here to judge or doubt any of those concerns because many of them are very real and can be somewhat difficult to navigate. But I can tell you for sure that there is always a way, always a pathway forward. It may be slower, it may take longer, it may be harder, but there is still *always* a path forward toward getting better.

A few years ago, while I was working on the ceiling in my shop, some scaffolding collapsed. I fell from a height of about 10 feet and landed on top of a beam on the floor, right on top of my shoulder, crushing it. With the help of good surgeons, physical therapists, and support from my family, I was able to obtain a recovery of nearly 100 % of my pre-trauma ability. Once the surgery was over, I immediately started going back to my regular routine, albeit with a few modifications. This is antifragility in action; not just bouncing back, but using the challenge to learn and grow stronger.

Injuries suck and simply take longer to recover from as we get older. However, did you know that if you injure one body part, you should continue working on the others? For example, even if your right shoulder is immobilized, if you continue to work the *left* shoulder, you will have less disuse atrophy (shrinking) in your *right* shoulder as it heals. This is amazing to me! There is some crossover benefit on the opposite side. This is why if my clients have an injury, I always tell them to continue "working" the other side. My reason for telling you all of this is that sometimes we come up with excuses for why we think we can't do things. In reality, they are just excuses, not reasons. There's a big difference.

I feel the need to share one more story here if you are still undecided whether all of this is worth the effort or not. There is a man in my family who has always struggled with health and wellness, and he means the world to me. He has tried on and off throughout the years to get "fit." When he was younger, he managed all of these setbacks because of the gift of youth. However, as he got older, it became a bigger and bigger problem. This is the trap a lot of older men fall into. It kinda sucks but not so much as to make you take action. The problem becomes— and I can't stress this enough—that when they finally get to the point where they *need* to do something, it is a gargantuan effort to regain health and vitality. The bottom line is that training is easy to do, but it is also easy *not* to do. I suggest that you always dig the well before you get thirsty!

"CARDIO" MYTHS

I know we already touched on this, but you need to fully commit this to memory. You *cannot* out-exercise poor nutrition or overeating—especially as we get older. It simply doesn't work. The main reason this never works is that chronic intense cardio will make you as hungry as a bear, so people always eat more after intense cardio because they think they "deserve" it. No, you don't. Just quit running endlessly and sweating your ass off on a treadmill. You may burn 400 calories, but then you eat 500 (or more!) The only cardio I recommend is daily walking—say 10,000 steps—at a fairly fast pace where you are breathing slightly harder than normal. (You should still be able to carry on a conversation.) You don't need to complete a full 10,000 steps if you are short on time, but set a goal and *do it daily*. 4,000 seems to be the absolute minimum number here to get most of the benefits.

I also like to do one HIIT (high intensity interval training) session per week. I like to do this on an exercise bike, but pick your poison (a rower or elliptical are fine too). I do not recommend older folks do a lot of running because you simply do not need to and it can be hard on knees and hips. HIIT works like this: After warming up, go all-out for 20-30 seconds. Then, rest for around 60 seconds.

Simply do that for six to ten repetitions. That's it; no more, no less. Pro tip: download the Tabata app and it will track these intervals for you. Yes, you will burn a few calories during the activity, but the main benefit is from something called EPOC. It stands for excess post-exercise oxygen consumption. Basically, HIIT can raise your basal metabolic rate, which means you burn more calories at rest *and* burn more calories while you are sleeping. What's not to love about that? Some evidence suggests this type of training can cause your body to produce more growth hormone as well.. Besides a daily walk, this is really all the "cardio" we need.

HIIT training has one more benefit, I call it DOSE. When you go all-out for a short time and then rest, you release more feel good hormones. D=Dopamine, O= Oxytocin, S=Seratonin, and E = Endorphins. This is why some people say exercise is the best anti-depressant available. Try it for yourself.

Still don't believe how important it is to not only maintain but build muscle as we age? There is a term for this now called "muscle-centric wellness." Muscle-centric wellness is an approach to health and well-being that emphasizes the importance of maintaining and optimizing muscle mass as a central component of overall health, especially as we age. This idea is based on the understanding that muscle is not just important for strength and mobility but also plays a crucial role in metabolic health, hormone regulation, immune function, and longevity.

*Obviously, consult your physician before starting any type of training regimen.

Key principles of muscle-centric wellness include:

1. **Muscle as the organ of longevity**: Muscle mass is associated with better health outcomes, including improved metabolic health, reduced risk of chronic diseases like diabetes, and enhanced quality of life in older age. (Notice I didn't say *old* age.)

2. **Focus on strength training**: Prioritize resistance training to build and maintain muscle, which in turn helps maintain metabolic function, mobility, and independence, particularly as people get older.

3. **Nutrition geared toward muscle maintenance**: Adequate protein intake is emphasized to support muscle growth and repair alongside balanced nutrition to support overall body function.

4. **Prevention of sarcopenia**: As we age, we naturally lose muscle mass in a process called sarcopenia. Muscle-centric wellness focuses on preventing/reversing or slowing down this loss to ensure vitality and independence.

5. **Holistic approach to health**: This approach acknowledges the connection between muscle health and other aspects of wellness, including bone density, cognitive function, and the ability to recover from injury or illness.

In essence, muscle-centric wellness suggests that by focusing on building and maintaining muscle, we can enhance overall health, improve longevity, and enjoy a better quality of life, particularly in later years.

One standout study published in BMC Geriatrics, 2022, conducted over a 12-year period, looked at the relationship between skeletal muscle mass (SMM) and mortality in older adults. The findings showed a clear association between lower levels of muscle mass and higher rates of mortality from all causes, including cardiovascular disease and cancer. Let me summarize the findings so they are relatable and understandable.

- **Low Skeletal Muscle Mass**: The study found that individuals with lower levels of muscle mass, as measured by dual-energy X-ray absorptiometry (DEXA scan), had a significantly higher risk of all-cause mortality. Muscle mass plays a key role in metabolic health, and the loss of lean muscle tissue can lead to a cascade of health problems, including insulin resistance, inflammation, and weakened immunity.

- **Impact on Physical Function**: The study also highlighted that poor physical performance—such as slow walking speed, low grip strength, and difficulty standing from a sitting position—was strongly correlated with increased mortality. Physical performance is often a direct reflection of muscle health, particularly in aging populations.

Let's not let it get to the point of being "difficult to stand from a sitting position," at least not until we get over 100, maybe we will get a pass then.

ANTIFRAGILE SLEEP AND RECOVERY

As we age, sleep becomes one of the most critical components of our overall health and resilience. Yet, it is often one of the first behaviors that go out the window as we enter the busy season of our lives. Sleep isn't just about rest as we age; it becomes one of the most critical components of our overall health and resilience. Yet, it's often the first thing we sacrifice in our busy lives. Sleep is the foundation of recovery, mental clarity, and physical strength. For the antifragile man, prioritizing sleep is non-negotiable.

So How Much Sleep Do We Need?

Most adults require 7-9 hours per night to function at their best, although the optimal amount of sleep varies. As we age, our sleep patterns may change, but the need for quality rest remains constant. Insufficient sleep impacts nearly every aspect of health, from metabolism to cognitive function, and even muscle recovery.

The Science of Sleep

One notable study published in Nature found that sleep deprivation affects more than 700 genes related to stress, immunity, and metabolism. Chronic lack of sleep has been linked to increased risks of heart disease, diabetes, obesity, and cognitive decline. Conversely, quality sleep enhances memory, reduces inflammation, and accelerates muscle repair—a cornerstone of antifragility.

Optimizing Sleep

Advancements in sleep technology make it easier to understand and improve your sleep. Devices like the Oura Ring provide insights into sleep stages, heart rate variability, and overall recovery. With this data, you can identify patterns and make changes to optimize your rest.

Consider implementing these strategies to enhance sleep and recovery:

- Create a Sleep Sanctuary: Keep your bedroom dark, cool (60-67°F), and quiet. Use blackout curtains and a white noise machine if needed. Be sure your mattress and pillow fit your preferences

- Stick to a Schedule: To regulate your body's internal clock, go to bed (preferably at the same time) and wake up at the same time every day, even on weekends.

- Mid-day napping can be helpful, but keep it short (10-30 minutes max). If you wake up groggy instead of refreshed, cut it back in 5-minute increments until you find your sweet spot.

- Try to get exposure to direct sunlight first thing in the morning. This resets your circadian rhythm

- Limit Screen Time: Avoid blue light from phones and screens for at least an hour before bed. Blue light disrupts melatonin production.

- Invest in Sleep Technology: Use devices like the Oura Ring or Whoop Band to track your sleep quality and recovery patterns.

- Avoid Stimulants: Limit caffeine and alcohol intake, especially in the afternoon and evening.

- Wind Down: Develop a pre-sleep routine, such as reading, stretching, or meditating, to signal to your body that it's time to relax.

- Support Your Circadian Rhythm: Get natural sunlight exposure during the day and minimize artificial light at night.

- Monitor Your Diet: Avoid heavy meals close to bedtime and consider magnesium or herbal teas like chamomile to aid relaxation.

- Train Regularly: physical work will make you tired and promotes deeper sleep. However, avoid intense workouts too close to bedtime (another example of how training *and* recovery are synergistic) because they could contribute to being more awake in the short-term.

ANTIFRAGILE TACTICS

- Do *something* physical every day. It doesn't have to be Navy SEAL training or taking hours at the gym every day. Just do a few sit-ups, pushups, and jumping jacks (remember those from gym class?) or whatever. Movement every day can transform your health

- Remember progressive overload, time under tension, and proper form

- Think you don't have time? Every time you tell someone you don't have time, you are really saying that thing is not important enough for you to make the time.

- Use what is available but lift heavy things (weights at the gym, rocks, propane bottles, bales of hay). Don't exercise the same body part on back to back days. As you progress, do more.

- Quit slogging away on the treadmill to burn calories! Remember EPOC and raise your metabolic rate to burn more calories at rest. Aim for 10,000 steps per day (or whatever goal you set)

- Physique can be enhanced more easily with "good" genetics, but "poor" genetics are far from a death sentence. Remember, Epigenetics (your environment) dictates gene expression.

- Drink your water (half your body weight in oz.)

- Explore supplements, but pick the low-hanging fruit like nutrition, sleep, and training first.

- Remember: abs are built in the kitchen, not the gym

- Be intentional here. Remember that we are training our unconscious mind at the same time. We are the kind of people who do what we said we would do.

- It is *imperative* that you understand that every day your body is breaking down (decaying) *and* building up. As we age, the tendency is toward more decay and less building up. The key here is to be sure there is more building up happening every day than there is breaking down (decay).

- Focus on muscle-centric wellness

PART 4

THRIVING IN RELATIONSHIPS, MASCULINITY, AND ABUNDANCE

CHAPTER 10

IT'S OKAY TO BE A MAN

Over the past few decades, as society has rightfully focused on empowering women, many men (young and old) have found themselves questioning their identity and purpose. To be clear, women most certainly need and deserve to be equal in every way to men. We are all better together, and women most certainly have their gifts to offer all of us, but men do as well. I have the most amazing wife/soulmate/life partner and two kickass, successful, powerful daughters, and a female dog. All of whom are priceless, and they teach me so many valuable lessons every day.

My goal is for men of all ages to embrace being stronger, wiser, and more fulfilled in life. Society needs positive male energy for a balanced and nurturing family environment. It shouldn't be a bad thing to open a car door for a lady. I still do that for my wife, and maybe that is why we have been together for 43 years. I recognize women are fully capable and strong enough to open their own doors, but what's the harm in showing that you care about and respect them? What about walking on the "traffic" side of the street and having them walk on the inside? It shows you value their safety..

I have found that many men are conflicted about their role in society. Our goal in being a strong and powerful man is not to use our power to make somebody else less powerful. We should climb the ladder of masculinity so we can lend a hand to others when we reach the top.

In recent years, the term "toxic masculinity" has gained traction in public discourse, often portraying traditional masculine traits as negative or harmful. While there are behaviors—such as aggression, suppression of emotions, or domination—that can be harmful when taken to extremes, labeling masculinity as "toxic" misrepresents the issue. It's not masculinity itself that is the problem, but the misuse or distortion of its traits. Unfortunately, media narratives often amplify the idea that toxic masculinity is pervasive, creating confusion and, at times, shame among men who struggle to understand where they fit in.

The truth is that healthy masculinity is a powerful force for good. Traits traditionally associated with masculinity—strength, resilience, courage, leadership, and a protective instinct—are invaluable when channeled productively. Men don't need to suppress their masculinity; they need to refine it. The key lies in embracing these traits while pairing them with kindness, compassion, and self-awareness.

To foster this balance, men should focus on developing emotional intelligence, building strong relationships, and living with integrity. Being a strong man doesn't mean being unyielding or domineering; it means standing firm in your values, protecting those you love, and being a positive role model. By rejecting the false narrative that masculinity is inherently harmful and embracing its positive aspects, men can reclaim their role as pillars of strength and stability in their families, communities, and society at large.

This chapter explores the importance of embracing masculinity in a world that often seems conflicted about the role of men. By understanding and celebrating the unique strengths and contributions of men, while also respecting and empowering women, we create a more balanced and Antifragile society as a whole. This chapter will provide insights into the challenges facing modern men, offering strategies for maintaining a strong male identity and encouraging a healthy balance between masculine and feminine energies. To become Antifragile in today's world, men must first understand and overcome the stereotypes and challenges they face.

CAVEMEN STEREOTYPES

Men have long battled reductive stereotypes—from the primitive caveman dragging women by their hair to the emotionally stunted brute incapable of complex feelings. These caricatures not only misrepresent men but also damage our understanding of gender roles and relationships.

Another huge problem I have seen is how some women feel the need to overcompensate or work harder than their male counterparts to get the same respect, especially on the job. Men need to be aware of this, and if you become aware of a lack of respect happening then just quit being that guy. Lack of respect for women doesn't help anybody and is counterproductive to any organization or group.

These stereotypes not only affect how men are perceived but also influence workplace dynamics between men and women. Rather than forcing men to choose between toxic hypermasculinity and the complete rejection of traditional male attributes, we should aim for an integrated approach to manhood. It's okay and necessary for men to be real men these days; it's also necessary to recognize that women have special talents that men don't. That's the way it is supposed to be—a symbiotic relationship where we use our talents and God-given gifts to help each other and all of humanity in the process.

We need men who embrace both strength and wisdom. During my years working as a bartender/bouncer in Montana bars to pay for college, I learned that true strength often prevents conflict rather than creates it. People who sensed my confidence and capability rarely challenged me. I never started fights, but I was prepared to resolve them when necessary. This experience taught me that genuine strength—physical, mental, and emotional—creates security and stability rather than chaos.

A good man isn't boastful about his strength or constantly trying to prove himself. Instead, he remains vigilant and aware; he maintains constant awareness of potential threats to those he cares about. His strength lies in his readiness and resolve, not in displays of dominance. Ask my sons-in-law if there was any ambiguity in my expectations about how they would treat my daughters—respect and protection are non-negotiable.

Here is one example of what I am talking about. Even though I agree with most of his policies, (heaven forbid) one of the most ridiculous things Donald Trump ever did was attack John McCain, who fought for our country. This is an example of confusing power with strength and bullying. I am glad to see that he is beginning to realize this after the most recent assassination attempt. Staring our mortality right in the face has a tendency to bring perspective to the forefront.

Conduct yourself with confidence and humility. Get your ego out of the way. It's been said that ego is the anesthesia that deadens the pain of stupidity! Not everything is about you. Think first about how your actions and/or comments may affect others. If something doesn't need to be said, then be a good man and say nothing.

PEACE THROUGH STRENGTH

A society with well-adjusted, strong men is necessary for a peaceful existence. I think this was painfully obvious during the riots we saw during the last few years here in the US. I am all for peaceful protest and the right of free speech. However, that sentiment doesn't mean it's okay to destroy other people's property and/or the businesses for which they have worked their whole lives. "Protest" and "riot" are two vastly different things.

Strong, well-adjusted men will stand up for themselves, their family, and even complete strangers when needed.. As a society, we all need to police ourselves and our own behavior better.

The challenges facing contemporary men differ dramatically from those of previous generations. During World War II, young men lied about their age to join the fight against fascism, driven by a clear sense of purpose and duty. Today's men navigate a much more complex social landscape where traditional roles are constantly questioned and redefined. This evolution has created legitimate confusion for many men about how to express their masculinity in ways that are both authentic to themselves and constructive for society.

STEROIDS AND HORMONES (BIOLOGICAL MANLINESS)

There's significant confusion surrounding the use of anabolic-androgenic steroids—or, in short, steroids. This section clarifies the big differences regarding steroid use and what has been dubbed

HRT (hormone replacement therapy). The term steroids is often used to refer to injecting artificial testosterone at artificially high doses for the sole purpose of growing muscle. In contrast, TRT refers to a medical intervention to balance all of the hormones to normal physiologic levels. This not only involves testosterone but also estrogen (yes, men need estrogen, too), progesterone, and dihydrotestosterone (DHT). A doctor trained in HRT will have an understanding of all of the individual hormones as well as their interconnectedness. If you decide to pursue HRT, finding a physician with specific training in hormonal balance is critical for safety and effectiveness.

This begs the question: How do steroids grow so much more muscle than just working out alone? The simplistic answer revolves around what is called protein synthesis. The difference is in the amount and duration of protein synthesis after a workout. If a person is using anabolic steroids, the protein synthesis will nearly double in about 24 hours. Simply working out "natty" (naturally and without performance-enhancing drugs), your increase in protein will last about 24-36 hours, but its peak will be nowhere near double. This is also why experts recommend not working out the same body part on back-to-back days.

It is estimated that a bodybuilder using "roids" can build more muscle in less than three months than a natty bodybuilder can in three years. Given our obsession with immediate gratification, it is no wonder that many men turn to illegal anabolic steroid use to grow bigger, faster. However, if you want to be Antifragile as you age, be careful. Misuse of anabolic steroids will eventually bite you in the ass due to the unwanted side effects and you will wish you had never heard of them. They simply aren't worth the risk. Just like a fake Rolex, nobody else may know but *you* do. Eventually, fake catches up with you. If not from the outside, it surely will affect you from the inside. Just do it the "hard" way, enjoy the suck, and be proud of the long term benefits.

Let's set a few things straight. Anabolic steroid use/abuse has been around for decades. Even the great Arnold Schwarzenegger admits to using them back in the day. I am not judging here, and it is safe to say that back in that day, we really did not know a lot about the long-term consequences of artificially high testosterone levels. Today, that is not the case. It is crazy to think about it, but back in "the day," some guys were actually injecting equine (yes, horse) steroids. They got crazy big and ripped, but the long-term consequences were devastating to their overall health. I had a lot of friends who used them when we were in our prime, and almost all of them regret it now. At the time, it was great for them because they got crazy big and strong, but eventually, if the muscles are artificially strong, the tendons, ligaments, and bones cannot keep up, and something has to give—hello, injuries!

I encourage any of you older chaps who feel weak and feel like your get-up-and-go got-up-and-went, to seek out an experienced Doc trained in HRT and at least get your levels tested. Doing that does not require you to do anything about it but, if it turns out you are low or off in any of your values, then at least consider your options. I know a lot of men who have benefited greatly from getting things back to normal levels.

Research indicates a concerning trend: testosterone levels in young men have been declining steadily for decades. This phenomenon deserves serious attention for its potential health implications.

In a 2020 study by Kristie L. Kahl and colleagues done at Yale University, (Urology Times, July 3, 2020.Volume 48.No7) this looming hormone problem was documented. The researchers looked at testosterone levels in adolescents and young adult men (AYA). From 1999 to 2000, levels of "T" were around 605 (ng/dl or nanogram per deciliter). From 2003-2004, this had declined to around 567 (ng/dl). From 2011-2012, it was about 425 (ng/dl). This represents a nearly 30% drop in just over a decade.

Multiple studies have confirmed this downward trend, which is particularly concerning because adolescence and early adulthood should represent peak testosterone production in males. The scientific community recognizes this as an urgent research priority, not simply for cultural reasons related to masculinity but because of the serious health implications. While definitive causes remain under investigation, several factors warrant consideration:

Low "T" levels correlate with higher rates of comorbidities (concurrent diseases) and increased all-cause mortality. This is likely due to poor diet, lack of exercise, higher percentage of body fat, stress, anxiety about our roles as males, and environmental toxins. The scientific literature suggests multiple potential contributors, including:

- Poor dietary patterns, particularly highly processed foods

- Sedentary lifestyle and insufficient resistance training

- Increasing obesity rates

- Environmental endocrine disruptors

- Chronic stress and disrupted sleep patterns

- Recreational drug use

MEN NEED TO TAKE RISKS FOR THE GREATER GOOD

Additional research found in David Gilmore's *Manhood in the Making* anthropological study examines masculinity across various cultures. It suggests that, despite many cultural differences, certain roles commonly appear in conceptions of masculinity across diverse cultures. These frequently include responsibility, protection, and provision—roles that have historically contributed to community survival and cohesion.

Gilmore studied cultures ranging from Mediterranean and South American societies to African tribes. He found that in nearly all groups, men are expected to protect their communities, provide for their families, and assume leadership roles during times of crisis. This sense of responsibility is not just social but deeply tied to a man's identity. Without these roles, men in many cultures risk social exclusion and personal disempowerment.

One of Gilmore's key findings is that these masculine roles are *not* inherently oppressive but rather crucial for the well-being of the community. Men are often called upon to take physical and emotional risks for the greater good, whether through hunting, defending the community, or assuming leadership in difficult times. These roles help ensure the stability, security, and prosperity of the group, contributing to a sense of collective responsibility.

Gilmore also highlights that in cultures where traditional masculine roles are diminished, the social structure tends to weaken, leading to a lack of purpose among men and, consequently, societal instability. His book suggests that a well-functioning society depends on the active participation of men in fulfilling these traditional roles—not in a domineering or oppressive way, but as protectors, providers, and leaders.

For men in the modern western world, where traditional roles are increasingly questioned or blurred, Gilmore's study reaffirms the importance of reclaiming purpose through responsibility and contribution to the community.

It needs to be emphasized that it is okay for men to need and ask for help. A lot of us were raised by well-meaning fathers who did not feel that way. Sure, it was fine to ask for help to change out the V-8 350 for a high-compression 396, but it was not acceptable to ask for help about personal matters or how to handle our emotions. The reason was likely because they didn't know the answers to those questions. This is a huge problem for so many men (veterans especially) to navigate.

An Antifragile man knows when he needs help and should *never* be afraid to ask for it. Needing help is *not* a sign of weakness; it is a sign of greatness to know when to just "figure it out" and when to ask for help. Realize that other men (and women for that matter) would be honored that you asked for their assistance. It is in our DNA to be helpful.

ANTIFRAGILE TACTICS

- Embrace being a man and recognize the importance of male energy in society

- Understand the term "toxic masculinity" and do *not* embrace this concept

- Strive for a balance between strength and humility

- Be aware of declining testosterone and the potential causes and consequences

- Consider getting your hormone levels checked, especially as you age. Be open to HRT (hormone replacement therapy) if needed, but avoid anabolic steroid use

- Engage in traditionally masculine activities without guilt, recognizing their importance for your (and society's) well-being

- Respect and empower women while also maintaining a strong male identity

- It is *not* a sign of weakness to ask for help

- Focus on being a good man rather than just a nice guy

Now that we've explored the importance of embracing masculinity and maintaining hormonal balance, let's dive into how these factors play into our overall health and wellness as we age. In the next chapter, we'll discuss specific strategies for staying physically and mentally sharp, building on the foundation of a strong male identity we've established here.

CHAPTER 11

LOVE AS STRENGTH: THE ANTIFRAGILE HEART

Love might seem like the last thing that belongs in a discussion about becoming antifragile. After all, doesn't love make us vulnerable? Expose our soft underbelly? Risk heartbreak?

Precisely. And that's exactly why it's essential.

Love is perhaps the ultimate antifragile force. It exposes vulnerabilities, yes, but when we embrace these vulnerabilities rather than suppress them, we develop remarkable strength. The man who risks loving deeply—himself, others, his work, his life—builds the capacity to transform every loss, heartbreak, and conflict into wisdom and deeper resilience. The antifragile man doesn't grow stronger despite love's challenges but because of them.

This chapter explores the critical role of love, particularly self-love, in becoming an Antifragile man. By understanding and embracing love in its various forms, you build stronger relationships, improve your mental health, and become more resilient in the face of life's inevitable challenges.

ALL YOU NEED IS LOVE

Men are hardwired for pursuit—we chase goals, challenges, and yes, relationships. But here's what most men miss: the neurochemical reward system in our brains is activated more powerfully by the pursuit itself than by achieving the goal. This explains the common letdown many men experience after finally reaching a major milestone. The Dopamine, Oxytocin, Serotonin, and Endorphin rush comes from the chase, not the capture.

The antifragile man learns to love the struggle itself. He embraces discomfort not as something to endure but as the very thing that makes him stronger. This isn't just about being an "adrenaline junkie"—it's about understanding that comfort breeds fragility while strategic stress builds resilience. Whether through physical challenges, intellectual rigor, or spiritual practice, the man who learns to love the process rather than fixate on outcomes develops true antifragility.

Many men avoid the very concept of self-love, fearing it makes them less masculine or seems egotistical. This creates a false dichotomy: how can a man be both strong (the protector, the provider, the one who pushes limits) and loving? The antifragile answer rejects this either/or thinking. Strength without love becomes brittle; love without strength becomes ineffective. The integration of both creates something more powerful than either alone.

This balance—strength infused with love—is the hallmark of the truly antifragile man. He loves his life, his body, his experiences, and the people around him without apology or hesitation. He understands that expressing genuine love isn't weakness but a demonstration of his security in his own masculinity.

After loving your spouse, children, parents, and friends for years, it is now your turn to begin to understand that you must love yourself first, before you can share that gift with others. If you do not have self-love within you, there is no way for you to authentically share it with others.

Self-love is the foundation of Antifragility. Men often tie their self-worth to external achievements (physicality, wealth, or career). Self-love isn't complacency; it is the recognition of self-worth despite aging, previous failures, or losses. A man who loves himself enough to pursue health, purpose, and his passions despite society's growing acceptance of a declining average becomes truly Antifragile. One could say self-love is the soil where Antifragility takes root.

One of the key indicators of whether you have unconditional love is your level of happiness. Happiness is the key. Happiness doesn't come from material things or experiences; it comes from the inside. Your happiness should not depend on anybody else, not even your wife, kids, or any other external factors. Happiness comes from inner peace.

So what is the best way to nurture self-love? It is through discipline and embodying Antifragility. Embrace the suck, learn from your mistakes, and, most importantly, develop your discipline muscle. Yes, discipline is like a muscle. You must break it down over and over to make it stronger.

If you have discipline in all that you do, you are exhibiting self-love in action. When you master this, you can lead the way for others—especially younger men. It's really hard to convince others that discipline is the key to success if you cannot walk the walk. It's kind of like the oxygen mask on an airplane, you have to put yours on first so that you can help others, especially the younger or more fragile people.

By all means, please be aware or intentional regarding your self-talk. Some studies reveal that for men nearly 75 percent of our self-talk is negative. How in the world could you ever become Antifragile if most of your self-talk is about how fragile you are, how terrible you are, and what a bad person you are? Remember, Antifragility is doubling down when things are not going your way, not shrinking away from it.

If a good friend of yours was going through a tough time, how would you help them? Would you be there for them, console them, and help them, or would you confirm that they were worthless? I hope the answer is the former. If your good friends are anything like mine (you know who you are), they would be there for me in a second, asking how they could help. So the question is, if you wouldn't turn your back on a friend, why in the hell would you turn your back on yourself?

Love often opens the door to deeper spiritual dimensions of life. This isn't about imposing specific religious beliefs—whether you connect with a concept of God, the universe, collective consciousness, or something else entirely isn't what matters. What matters is recognizing how love can transcend our limited self-concepts and connect us to something larger.

Many men resist spiritual exploration precisely because it requires vulnerability—that perceived weakness they've been conditioned to avoid. Yet this exploration often leads to what might be the ultimate antifragile perspective: a relationship with mortality itself. When a man faces the inevitability of death through the lens of love rather than fear, he develops a remarkable freedom. This isn't about denying death's reality but transforming our relationship with it. The antifragile man doesn't just accept mortality; through love, he uses this awareness to live with greater purpose and presence.

Our creator looks at you as their child, their prodigy, and an outward expression of love, the same way you view your own children. You are that child, that perfect being (yes, we all have our gifts and flaws), but we must love ourselves as our creator loves us. Love yourself enough to be disciplined, do the work, and pursue your passions. Only when we love ourselves fully can we have any abundance to share with others.

Another expression of self-love is to answer the question: do you *always* do what you said you would do? Is your word your law? If you say you are going to start meditating, do it. If you are going to start working out regularly, do it! If you are not going to follow through, don't say you will.

By following through, you accomplish two things: First, you begin to be more intentional with your words. Second, you begin to train your mind that when you say you will do something, you do it. The side effect is that you begin to establish credibility with other people, and they will definitely respond more positively the next time you have an interaction with them.

Love for others nurtures Antifragile communities. It always seems crazy to me how independence is encouraged, yet in reality, isolation will kill you. Love from family, communities and friends allows us to create a web of support and assures we don't break when the shit hits the fan.

People are uncannily adept at spotting phony behavior, so you must be genuine. Treat everyone as if they have a sign on the front of their T-shirt that says, "Please make me feel important." You will be amazed how this seemingly simple shift in awareness will change their life and yours!

When I observe someone acting peculiar, I ask myself, "I wonder what happened to that person to make them that way" instead of "I wonder what is wrong with that person." It is amazing what happens to your energy when you approach life this way. We have all been through things that have permanently changed us mentally and/or physically. This may make us different from what society deems "normal," but when you get to know most of these people, it is a wonder they have survived, let alone thrive.

THE IMPORTANCE OF LISTENING

Learn to ask better questions and be a better listener. Remember, we have two ears and one mouth, so use them in that order of importance. Learn to be *interested*, rather than interesting. Be genuinely interested in other people's stories.

Oftentimes, you will be blown away when you actually listen to people and understand where they are coming from and the things, both good and bad, that they have experienced. I will admit I did not always understand this, but when I learned to do this with intention, I was shocked to learn things I never knew, even about close friends. Oftentimes, people are so desperately wanting to prove to people how smart or important they are that they don't listen. Instead, they think about how to respond and impress people. It is not endearing or impressive to be the person who always has a "better" or more impressive story. To the contrary, doing this will more often alienate you from the other person. Nobody wants to hang around someone who is perfect or, worse, someone who *thinks* they're perfect. One of my mentors put it this way: "Perfection is neurotic; excellence is inspirational."

Random acts of kindness have a ripple effect. If you do something nice for someone else, your levels of feel-good hormones increase. Hormones like serotonin (associated with healing), oxytocin (often called the love hormone), and endorphins (that decrease pain) all skyrocket as a result of random acts of kindness. The recipient of the kindness also has their feel-good hormones increase. But here is the crazy part, the *observer* (people across the room) of random acts of kindness also experience a remarkable increase in their levels of these hormones.

This information absolutely confirms what we have intuitively understood for years. Namely, it makes us feel really good about helping others; it is innate in all of us. This is why it is so rewarding to volunteer in some capacity. We get so caught up in taking care of ourselves and our families that we forget how much these random acts of kindness can mean.

Simple things like smiling at someone can change your day, their day, and the day of others observing you smile. Why not smile? It is a lot easier than frowning. Remember, I was a Dentist. I know that it takes 47 muscles to frown but only 13 to smile, so why not make it easy on yourself?

Think about the effect that random acts of kindness could have on the world. If you and I practice them daily and we make a few other people happy or feel understood, and then, they do the same thing, an exponentially profound positive effect occurs. So please, when you are out interacting with other people, take a second, quit shoving your face in your phone, and say hello, smile, and give someone a genuine compliment. The world will be a better place and you will be happier.

Love is a oneness; it is a blurring of the line between you and me. What I desire most for me, I also desire for you! When you truly embody this, your whole life will change.

ANTIFRAGILE TACTICS

- Start with self-love as the foundation for loving others

- Cultivate happiness from within, not from external sources

- Develop discipline as a form of self-love and a path to Antifragility

- Be mindful of your self-talk and treat yourself with the same kindness you'd show a friend

- Keep your word and follow through on commitments to build self-respect and credibility

- Love can lead to a spiritual awakening

- Practice active listening and genuine interest in others' stories

- Engage in random acts of kindness to boost your own well-being and create a positive ripple effect.

- Love can be the ultimate Antifragile expression

- The Antifragile man grows stronger not despite love's risks, but because of them

Now that we've explored the power of love and its crucial role in becoming Antifragile, let's turn our attention to how we can apply these principles in our daily lives. In the next chapter, we'll discuss practical strategies for integrating love, discipline, and kindness into our routines, relationships, and personal growth journey.

CHAPTER 12

THE LAW OF ABUNDANCE

You can have or be anything you want in life, I promise you. However, many of us have had or will have imposter syndrome (as previously discussed in Chapter 5). We question ourselves: Who am I to have such an amazing life? I am just a regular guy, so why would I think I am anything "special?"

When most men confront failure, they respond in one of two ways: they either retreat into scarcity thinking ("I never had a chance") or they harden themselves against the possibility of future failure ("I'll never try that again"). Both reactions create fragility. But what if failure wasn't a signal to retreat or harden, but an invitation to expand? This is where the Law of Abundance becomes crucial to the Antifragile man

This chapter explores how to embrace abundance for a more fulfilling and Antifragile life. By understanding abundance and overcoming limiting beliefs about success and money, you can unlock your potential for growth and prosperity. You'll discover how abundance isn't just an outcome you pursue, but a practice that transforms how you respond to every challenge life presents.

At first glance, abundance (the idea that there is limitless opportunity, wealth, health, and success available) and antifragility (growing stronger from adversity) might seem like separate concepts. But examine them closely, and you'll find they operate on the same fundamental principle: expansion under pressure.

The fragile man sees resources as finite and guards what he has. When pressure comes, he breaks. The resilient man endures pressure without breaking but returns to his original state. But the antifragile man? He expands under pressure - and this expansion is only possible through an abundance mindset.

Abundance isn't just about receiving more; it's about becoming a person who can handle more. Men who avoid stress (emotional, financial,or physical) remain fragile and unknowingly resist abundance because they are not prepared for it. The opposite of an abundance mindset is one of scarcity. This occurs when you think in terms of limited resources, as if someone else's wealth means less potential for prosperity exists for you, but that's not the case. A scarcity mindset is a breeding ground for fragility. This is linked to a fear of failure, and a fear of failure keeps good men from taking actions that lead to abundance. They often fail to recognize that success (in business, health, or relationships) is a game of repetitions.. Within reason, the more risks you take, the more opportunities that can show up in your life.

OVERFLOWING WITH ABUNDANCE

The life you're living today results from choices you made months or years ago. This isn't random chance or cosmic punishment - it's the harvest principle at work. The antifragile man understands this deeply: today's abundance or scarcity reflects yesterday's decisions and actions.

Most men struggle with this principle because they've been conditioned for immediate feedback. But real transformation operates on a different timeline. The business you build today might not show profits for a year. The investment you make now might not mature for a decade. The relationship skills you develop might take months to transform your marriage.

This delayed feedback loop creates a critical filter: it separates those who truly believe in abundance from those who merely like the idea of it. When you plant seeds of abundance through consistent action without immediate reward, you're demonstrating authentic belief in the principle.

Having an abundance mindset will bring out skepticism for many, but if you adopt this philosophy and work with it, good things will eventually come your way. I've witnessed this transformation repeatedly in my own life and in the lives of men I've mentored. One of the reasons some people think this is hogwash is because they think that they are just victims and have no control over their lives. They think things just happen, and they are reactive as opposed to proactive.

Another common objection comes from the zero-sum fallacy: "If I gain abundance, someone else must lose it." This scarcity thinking reveals a fundamental misunderstanding about how value creation works. The most successful entrepreneurs don't take slices of an existing pie - they bake entirely new pies. When you create genuine value, you can simultaneously increase your own abundance while improving others' lives.

People who adopt a victim mentality were likely taught those ideas at a young age. The law of abundance doesn't mean you can simply say to yourself, "I have abundance," and then just sit on the couch and wait for it to show up. On the contrary, you still have to do some kind of work to get any reward, but if you adopt an abundant mindset and focus on it, good things will eventually come your way. Just as we talked about limiting beliefs, whatever you focus on, you will get more of.

IT'S WHAT YOU DO WITH THE MONEY THAT COUNTS

Let's address abundance in regards to money. Money is an excellent test of a man's relationship with abundance and his capacity for antifragility.

Many of us have a negative view of money and what it signifies. These beliefs are usually instilled in us by well-meaning parents.

The adults who said money is evil were simply misinformed, quite likely by their own well-meaning parents. As discussed in Chapter 5, money is simply an exchange of energy—a thank-you note. If you provide enough value in the marketplace, you will be rewarded accordingly.

Money functions as an amplifier of your existing character. If you're generous with $100, you'll likely be generous with $100,000. If you are a good person, more money will make you an even better person. If you are an asshole, it will make you an even bigger asshole. Money doesn't change your character; it reveals and magnifies it.

We all know people who don't have a lot of money but are nonetheless extremely giving, happy, and fulfilled. Years ago, I took my entire dental team to Mexico and built houses for people who were living in "homes" made of pallets covered with blankets on a dirt floor. By an American standard of living, these people were poor and powerless.. The funny thing is that they were also happy, kind, and clean.

My wife Kelly was amazed how the women had clean, brightly colored clothing, yet they had no running water and lived in a structure with a dirt floor. When we peeked inside some of these dwellings, we would usually see three or four mattresses on the dirt floor and not much else. There was no pantry or food supply. These people lived day to day, but they were well-adjusted. The men wanted to work, but if they left to go to a job, they would come back to an empty home— all of their possessions would be gone. They didn't have much, but they needed to keep what they had.

When we completed a house, we would take the lucky family inside to show them around. By U.S. standards, even these shelters were pretty basic, but they had a door to lock, windows to open and close, a concrete floor, running water, a clothes washer, and a dishwasher. It was bizarre to witness grown adult women observing the wonders of a dishwasher and a vacuum cleaner for the first time. Even something as simple as a mirror in the bathroom was fascinating to them. Most of these people had never seen themselves in a mirror.

What struck me most was their antifragile relationship with possessions. When you own almost nothing, you develop a remarkable capacity to adapt and find joy independent of material comfort. These families demonstrated an antifragility that many wealthy Americans have lost - they had developed internal resources that couldn't be taken from them, even when external resources were scarce.

By contrast, I know *many* people who are wealthy by anyone's definition, yet they have a miserable attitude.. They drain your energy when you are around them. They live in amazing houses, drive beautiful new cars, and take amazing vacations. None of it does anything for them. They are grumpy and no fun to be around. These are the folks who are in Hawaii on a beautiful beach, staying in a five-star resort and complain because the sun is too hot, their $150 dollar Wagyu ribeye was more medium than medium rare, or their Manhattan wasn't swirled properly. Their fragility is evident in how easily their happiness is disrupted by minor inconveniences—the wrong temperature on an expensive steak, a slightly imperfect cocktail, or too much sunshine on their luxury vacation. They've optimized for comfort rather than capacity. Consequently, they have become fragile to even the smallest disruptions. Living with abundance isn't about the money. It is about what you do with the money that matters most.

Earlier, I mentioned that people shouldn't want to make a million dollars simply to make a million dollars. Rather, I think you want to make a million dollars (or whatever sum you think is a lot) to become the kind of person you have to become to make a million dollars. This way, you know the value of that money, and you have made yourself a better, more valuable person in the marketplace. If, for some reason, you lose the money or it gets taken away, you still have the ability and skill set to get more. That is how you live with an abundance mindset.

If you live a nice life, enjoy the money, and avoid excesses, you will be fulfilled in every way. The people I know who have done well for themselves and are genuinely happy use their excess money to do something nice and impactful for others. They reach a hand back down, which is different from a hand out. People, in general, with their hand out usually want something for nothing, which doesn't end well for anybody. People who know how to live with abundance know the difference and will give the shirt off of their back to help someone who genuinely needs help. What a beautiful feeling it is to help someone in need. However, if you do not have any excess yourself, you cannot help anyone else.

ANTIFRAGILE TACTICS

- Embrace the Law of Abundance and believe in unlimited opportunities

- The Antifragile man doesn't chase abundance, he creates the right conditions for abundance to be attracted to him by becoming the kind of man who can handle, sustain, and multiply it

- Understand that success often comes from consistent effort over time, not overnight

- You have to be ready to receive (in your heart) abundance as well, a lot of people struggle with this thinking they are not "worthy".

- Adopt an abundant mindset, but remember that work is still required to achieve results

- Recognize that money is neutral; it simply amplifies who you already are

- True wealth is not just about money but about the person you become and how you use your resources

- Happiness and fulfillment can and should exist independently of material wealth

- Stop waiting for "perfect" conditions; act now! Launch that business, take that risk, and start that conversation

- Track both failures and successes, they are both a part of your Antifragile expansion

- Strive to achieve financial abundance so you can help others and make a positive impact

Now that we've explored the concept of abundance and its role in creating an Antifragile life, let's turn our attention to how we can apply these principles in our daily lives and financial decisions. In the next chapter, we'll discuss practical strategies for cultivating an abundance mindset and using our resources to create lasting value for ourselves and others.

CHAPTER 13

HOPE FOR THE FUTURE

What if the final third of your life could be the most rewarding, vibrant, and meaningful part of your life? This isn't wishful thinking—it's becoming increasingly possible. At this stage, we possess hard-earned wisdom and perspective that only decades of experience can provide. And if current trends in longevity research continue, we're approaching a fascinating inflection point: live just five more years, and you may benefit from exponentially better health technologies that could extend your life by another decade... and then another.

This chapter explores the exciting possibilities for the future of longevity and health, offering hope and practical strategies for becoming Antifragile as we age. By understanding emerging technologies, embracing beneficial stressors, and taking proactive steps in our health management, we can extend our healthspan and challenge the concept of aging.

WHERE WILL YOU BE FIVE YEARS FROM NOW?

The decisions you make today will shape your future decades from now. We often get caught in short-term thinking. We're trying to make it through the work week, manage that nagging knee pain, or reach the next milestone. But this chapter invites you to lift your gaze further into the horizon and think about things beyond today, tomorrow, or the next week. What kind of life do you want in five, ten, or twenty years? Contrary to common belief, your future health isn't predetermined by your age or genetics; it's being actively shaped by your daily choices.

Ray Kurzweil serves as Google's Director of Engineering and is one of the world's leading futurists. He talks about something called "longevity escape velocity." Basically, he's saying that by 2028-2030, our life expectancy might start improving faster than we're aging. It's like we're in a race with Father Time, and for once, we might be gaining on the old bastard. While eternal life remains in the realm of science fiction, the prospect of adding healthy decades to our lives is becoming increasingly plausible.

Tony Robbins has some interesting ideas about this stuff, too. He's talking about how if we can just hang on for a few more years, we might actually be able to put aging on pause. Sounds like science fiction, right? Well, so did the iPhone back in the day, and look where we are now. We're carrying around more computing power in our pockets than NASA had when it put a man on the moon. So don't be too quick to dismiss this stuff. We now see laparoscopic surgery as the norm, right? Yet it wasn't that many years ago that this alone would have been crazy to even think about. To be able to do a complicated surgery through a tiny hole in the skin, instead of a huge incision that took weeks or longer to heal, was considered impossible, but it is now done on a regular basis. Imagine what else will become the norm."

We can't wait for science to save us. We need to do our part. This is where the concept of Antifragility becomes essential. We need to actively prepare our bodies and minds to not just survive longer but to thrive as we age.

COLD SHOWERS AND ICY CREEKS

There's something called hormesis—a fancy word for "what doesn't kill you makes you stronger." Basically, a little bit of stress can be good for you and make you tougher. Cold therapy (cryotherapy) is one way to do this. However, you don't need to do anything extreme. Simply finishing your morning shower with 30-60 seconds of cold water can trigger beneficial physiological responses that strengthen your body over time.

Speaking of cold, I learned about cryotherapy the hard way. I was in the middle of nowhere in Montana, with six horses, four guys, and enough gear to sink a battleship. It was absolutely frigid by the time we got out of our hunting camp, and to the neighbors basecamp where we had left a vehicle. All was good but the worst (for me) was yet to come.. Guess who got to ride the horses back home, up the river? That's right; yours truly.

Now, this wasn't a leisurely trot down a sunny trail. It was pitch black and below zero, and the trip back included seven creek crossings. Every one of them felt like a mini ice bath. Every time the water splashed up, it soaked through my jeans and chaps, freezing almost instantly. By the third crossing, I couldn't feel my feet. By the fifth, I wondered if I would ever feel them again. To add to the difficulty, the horses were about as eager to be outside at that time as I was, so they weren't exactly in a cooperative mood. They were cold and tired and could smell home. Every time we met one of those creeks, it was like trying to get a bunch of four-legged children to go to the dentist. From personal experience, I can tell you that was no easy task for many parents. The horses splashed and snorted through every creek. I was just trying to hold on and keep all of us moving in the right direction without going face-down in the ice bath.

By the time I got home, I was basically a popsicle with a pulse. Nonetheless, I had to take care of the horses before I could even think about warming up. Talk about hormetic stress! Once I got the horses settled and was finally able to get myself warm, I felt like a million bucks. That's the magic of hormesis. A little (or a lot) of suffering can do wonders. It's like your body thinks, "Holy shit, we survived that? We better toughen up in case this idiot tries to freeze us again."

Then there is the opposite—heat therapy. Heat shock proteins are the real deal. This is another form of hormesis that helps us build Antifragility. The health benefits of heat therapy have been intuitively understood for hundreds if not thousands of years. I was shocked when we toured Pompeii in Italy to find the elaborate saunas they had set up. These would have put the high end spas in Las Vegas to shame. The gold standard these days is infrared sauna. I personally love mine.

THE EVOLVING ROLE OF TECHNOLOGY ON ANTIFRAGILITY

Here are a few exciting developments that are reshaping what it means to age and live fully, providing real reasons to have hope for a vibrant, healthy, and purposeful future. Understand that this is by no means an exhaustive list of what's coming, but here are some highlights:

1. REGENERATIVE MEDICINE AND STEM CELL THERAPY

- **What is it?**: Regenerative medicine is revolutionizing how we think about aging by harnessing the body's own healing capabilities. Stem cell therapy, in particular, allows for the repair and regeneration of damaged tissues, including muscle, joints, and even organs.

- **Why it's exciting**: This technology offers older men the chance to recover from injuries and illnesses that previously led to physical decline. Imagine being able to repair worn-out cartilage in your knees and hips or revitalize aging heart tissue, extending not just lifespan but *healthspan* . As research progresses, stem cell therapy will continue to offer new avenues for maintaining physical vitality well into old age.

2. SENOLYTICS: TARGETING AGING AT THE CELLULAR LEVEL

- **What is it?** Senolytic drugs target and eliminate senescent cells, which are cells that have stopped dividing but remain in the body, contributing to inflammation and aging. These "zombie cells" are a major factor in age-related decline.

- **Why it's exciting**: By removing senescent (worn-out) cells, scientists believe we can slow down or even reverse certain aspects of the aging process. Early trials in humans are promising, and these drugs could soon offer a way to keep your body functioning at its best, allowing you to remain active and vital for decades longer than experts previously thought possible.

3. PERSONALIZED MEDICINE AND GENOMICS

- **What is it?** With the advancements in genomic sequencing, personalized medicine allows treatments to be tailored to your unique genetic makeup. This means you can receive therapies specifically designed for your body's needs, from nutrition to exercise to disease prevention.

- **Why it's exciting**: This highly individualized approach increases the effectiveness of medical treatments while minimizing side effects. Imagine a future where your doctor uses your genetic blueprint to optimize your diet, prevent illness, and design personalized exercise plans that maximize your physical health as you age. No more "one size fits all" approaches.

4. ARTIFICIAL INTELLIGENCE AND PREDICTIVE HEALTHCARE

- **What is it?** Artificial intelligence and machine learning are rapidly transforming how we approach challenges in life, including health, wellness, and personal growth. These technologies can empower us to make better decisions, optimize our health, and even adapt to unforeseen changes, helping us become more Antifragile. By analyzing vast amounts of data, AI can uncover patterns we may overlook, offering personalized solutions for longevity and resilience. AI-powered systems can analyze vast amounts of data from medical records, wearable devices, and genetic information to offer personalized recommendations for maintaining health. We are already seeing this play out within the field of radiology, where machine learning is advancing by leaps and bounds. People talk about getting second and third opinions regarding their health. Imagine if you could get thousands of opinions in the blink of an eye without ever leaving your couch.

- **Why it's exciting**: AI has the potential to catch diseases like cancer or heart disease years before symptoms appear, giving you a head start in preventing or treating them. As these systems become more advanced, older men will have unprecedented control over their health, allowing for more proactive, preventative healthcare strategies. I recently had a special type of CT scan that was sent to a company that has an AI algorithm to reconstruct an image of existing vascular plaques and predict the likelihood of them becoming a problem (i.e., A potential heart attack).

5. GENE EDITING WITH CRISPR

- **What is it?** CRISPR technology allows scientists to "edit" genes, correcting mutations that cause disease or enhancing certain genetic traits. This powerful tool could eventually be used to slow or stop the aging process at the genetic level. Inherited a bad gene sequence? Just cut it out and replace it with the correct one.

- **Why it's exciting**: CRISPR holds the potential to eliminate age-related diseases like Alzheimer's, heart disease, and diabetes, allowing for a healthier, longer life. Although we are still in the early stages of using CRISPR for anti-aging, the future looks bright for harnessing this technology to extend healthy human lifespans.

6. CONTINUOUS MONITORING WITH WEARABLE HEALTH TECH

- **What is it?** Wearable devices such as smartwatches, Oura rings, and fitness trackers are already commonplace, but new advancements are turning them into continuous health monitors. These devices can track heart rate, sleep quality, blood oxygen levels, and even glucose levels in real time.

- **Why it's exciting**: With continuous monitoring, men can make real-time adjustments to their lifestyle, catching early signs of trouble before they escalate into serious health issues. This empowers you to take control of your health and make informed decisions about your body every day, ensuring longevity and quality of life. These devices can also collect data from entire populations, helping to define what is "normal" and "abnormal" for a certain population. This can help doctors make individualized recommendations for your future.

7. ADVANCES IN MENTAL HEALTH AND COGNITIVE ENHANCEMENT

- **What is it?** New approaches to cognitive health, including nootropics (cognitive enhancers), brain stimulation techniques, and mindfulness practices like meditation are helping people maintain and even improve their mental acuity as they age.

- **Why it's exciting**: Cognitive decline is one of the biggest fears of aging, but emerging therapies and tools are offering real hope. Nootropics can enhance focus and memory. Mindfulness and meditation are proven to boost neuroplasticity, keeping the brain flexible and resilient. This means that aging men can stay sharp and continue contributing their wisdom and experience to their families and communities.

8. RAISING HUMAN CONSCIOUSNESS AND SPIRITUAL AWAKENING

- **What is it?** Beyond the physical and technological advancements, there is a growing movement focused on raising human consciousness. In addition to meditation, breath-work and psychedelics (used in controlled therapeutic settings) are being studied for their potential to foster spiritual growth, emotional resilience, and mental well-being.

- **Why it's exciting:** This elevation of consciousness offers a profound sense of purpose and connection. By embracing spiritual practices, men can experience greater peace, emotional strength, and a deeper understanding of themselves, which enriches their journey into the later stages of life. Antifragility is not exclusively about maintaining physical health; it's also about mental wellness and spiritual vitality. These practices, along with accumulated wisdom, may help us begin to understand that we are all connected on a much deeper level than we previously thought.

9. THE PROMISE OF LONGEVITY RESEARCH AND HUMAN LIFESPAN EXTENSION

- **What is it?** Research into lifespan extension, including calorie restriction mimetics, autophagy (the body's way of cleaning out damaged cells), and longevity drugs like rapamycin, is paving the way for humans to live longer, healthier lives.

- **Why it's exciting**: Scientists are increasingly optimistic about extending human lifespans, not just in terms of years but also regarding the quality of those years (i.e., your healthspan). If these interventions can significantly delay the aging process, then men in their 60s, 70s, and beyond could continue to live vibrant, purposeful lives with the energy to pursue new goals and dreams.

CONTINUE THRIVING

These advancements represent the tip of the iceberg when it comes to what's possible for aging men in the coming decades. The future is not just about surviving; it's about *thriving*. With breakthroughs in medicine, technology, and consciousness, older men can look forward to a future filled with vitality, purpose, and fulfillment. The last third of your life can and should truly be the best third. All of the lessons learned from our bumps and bruises combined with advanced technologies will help us emerge as Antifgragile men. Future generations may never get to experience life the same way we have been able to. Imagine the lessons we can share with those who never really had to "struggle" like we have. This is the essence of wisdom. If you really think about it, the struggle is what we crave because when we prevail it fills us up, and when we fall short, we learn.

The future's looking bright, but we must do our part. That means we should embrace discomfort and try new things. Some of you may be thinking you are too old to use these things to your advantage. Maybe you think technology is only for the young, and you view it as a threat instead of a tool. You couldn't be more wrong.

A lot of people these days are afraid of AI, but we will apply our Antifragile principles to embrace it. You should view AI as a way to multiply and amplify wisdom, not replace it.

The Antifragile man doesn't only survive amidst new technologies, he grows stronger by embracing them. He turns each advance into an opportunity to extend life, expand wisdom, and enhance his legacy. Technology evolves, and so must we.

A YOUTHFUL MIND PLUS WISDOM EQUALS ANTIFRAGILITY

Remember, we're in this for the long haul. With a little luck and a lot of grit, we might just outrun old Father Time for a while longer. The goal is not just to live longer but to live *a better, more vibrant, and fulfilled life.*

ANTIFRAGILE TACTICS

- Embrace the wisdom and experience that comes with age

- Stay informed about emerging longevity technologies and treatments

- Experiment with hormetic stressors like cold/heat therapy to build resilience

- Don't neglect regular medical check-ups and preventive care

- Be open to new health strategies, but approach them with common sense

- Recognize that small, consistent actions can have significant long-term health benefits

- Maintain a sense of humor and perspective about the aging process

- Remain vibrant and strong until these new things become available

- Remember that technology will continue to evolve, and so must we

Now that we've explored the exciting possibilities for extending our healthspan and even challenging the concept of aging itself, let's turn our attention to practical, everyday strategies for implementing these ideas. In the conclusion, we'll discuss how to integrate these future-focused health concepts into your daily routine, helping you become more Antifragile and prepared for whatever the future may bring.

BECOMING THE ANTIFRAGILE MAN

Alright boys, we've been on one hell of a journey together. We've talked about everything from embracing our age to kicking Father Time's ass. It's time to put it all together and answer the big question: what kind of man are you really going to be in the final third of your life? An Antifragile badass or a fragile has-been talking about how good you used to be? The choice is yours, and the time to decide is *now*. And remember, doing nothing is a choice as well. I suggest you choose wisely.

This book has shown you how to become an Antifragile man—someone who doesn't just survive the challenges of aging, but actually gets stronger because of them. We've explored how to embrace wisdom, redefine retirement, navigate the modern world, and overcome the mental barriers holding you back. Once you understand and implement these concepts, you'll be prepared to reach your goal—thriving in your "golden" years, not merely existing.

WHAT HAVE WE LEARNED?

In Chapter 1, we discussed embracing the age of wisdom. We talked about how getting older isn't a curse but an opportunity to leverage our hard-earned wisdom and experience. This set the stage for our journey into becoming Antifragile men.

Chapters 2 and 3 focused on redefining the back 9 of life and navigating modernity. We busted the myth that retirement means sitting on your ass. I mentioned suggestions about how to find new purpose and identity. We also tackled how to stay relevant and thrive in a world that's changing faster than a jackrabbit on a hot griddle.

In Chapters 4 and 5, we simplified nutrition and training. We cut through the BS, and I gave straightforward advice on fueling the body optimally and keeping it strong *without* killing ourselves in the gym. These chapters laid the foundation for physical Antifragility.

Chapters 6 and 7 dove deep into the mental game. We exposed the potential limiting beliefs holding us back, and I mentioned how to become aware of and overcome imposter syndrome and self-sabotage, as well as develop a healthy money mindset. This mental work is crucial for becoming truly Antifragile.

In Chapter 8, I showed how to set proper expectations for the future, getting our heads on straight about what's coming, and instructions on how to prepare. This led to Chapter 9, where we reclaimed what it means to be a man in today's world *without apology*.

Chapter 10 talked about love. Understanding and embracing love—for ourselves and others—is crucial for becoming Antifragile. Allowing yourself to be open and vulnerable to love is one of life's greatest lessons and joys. This tied into Chapter 11, where we explored the Law of Abundance and discussed how to shift from a scarcity mindset to one of abundance.

In Chapter 12, I painted a picture of hope for the future, showing the exciting possibilities ahead and why we should be excited about them. View AI as a tool and not a threat. It should be embraced to amplify wisdom.

Finally, Chapter 13 laid out an action plan with concrete steps to put all this knowledge into action and become the Antifragile man we're meant to be.

NOW WHAT ARE YOU GONNA DO?

At the beginning of the book, I asked you to write down five things you are excited about and five things you are apprehensive about in the final third of your life. I hope this book has brought more clarity to that list. Hopefully, you can now revise that list with the new information you've been given. My wish for you to recognize the excitement that awaits and take action on it!

Take control and create a "reserve capacity." You might ask, "What is this, and why would I want it?" At some point in your journey here on earth, you will get blindsided by something or someone you never saw coming. If that hasn't happened yet, consider yourself lucky. If you are weak and haven't prepared yourself, this alone could close the curtains for you—lights out. If you create a reserve capacity, when these things inevitably hit, you will have a much better chance of bouncing back, often without so much as a hair out of place.(for those of you that still have hair that is)

Antifragile men do not blame others. It is disrespectful to our creator and our families to not do everything in our power to thrive, so don't go down without a fight.

Remember, words matter. Focus on what you're grateful for. No matter what your situation is, it can always be worse.

Today is the youngest you will ever be. Just being born is a terminal illness, and none of us are getting out of this alive. Be cognizant of your own mortality.

Are you ready to embrace the suck, challenge yourself, and become the kind of man who doesn't just grow old, but grows better? 'The view from this side of life is great. And with what's coming down the pike, it might just get a whole lot better.

STAY CONNECTED.

If you are interested in working with us,
scan the QR code below

- You can join our Brotherhood at GeneTough.com

Follow us on

- Instagram: @GeneTough

- Facebook: facebook.com/GKtynes

- YouTube: @GeneToughTV

Now, who's ready for an ice-cold beer? After all, we gotta practice that cold therapy somehow, right? Cheers to the future, boys. May we all be around to see it, and may we be Antifragile enough to make the most of it.

ACKNOWLEDGMENTS

Writing *The Antifragile Man* has been one of the most demanding and deeply fulfilling endeavors of my life. It stretched me mentally, emotionally, and spiritually—but it was never a solo mission. This book stands on the shoulders of those who've walked beside me, believed in me, and pushed me to keep going when it would've been easier to quit.

First, to my wife and Soulmate Kelly—the love of my life, my compass, and my anchor—thank you for standing by me through every reinvention, every moment of doubt, and every early morning where this book came before the "fun" stuff. Your faith in me has never wavered. You are, and always will be, my greatest source of strength.

To my daughters, Sadie and Heidi—you are the embodiment of grace and resilience. Watching you grow into the strong, brilliant women you are today continues to inspire me. I hope this book reminds you, and your children, that life gets richer, deeper, and more powerful when we lean into challenge instead of running from it.

To my Son's-in-law, Jack and Mike—I am counting on you to not only live by these principles but also share them with the young men you encounter in the future.

To my grandkids—Theo, Tyne, Zoey, and RubyGene—may this book serve as a legacy you can draw strength from long after I'm gone. You are the future, and I write these words with the hope that they help guide you in whatever storms you face.

To my longtime clients, friends, and brothers and sisters in the Genetough program, thank you for trusting me with your stories, your goals, and your transformations. You've reinforced for me that age is not a limit—it's a launchpad. Your grit and growth breathe life into every principle in this book.

To my mentors, advisors, and early readers—thank you for your honesty, encouragement, and wisdom, especially my book "Guru" Charlie Hoehn. Your feedback shaped this book into something I'm truly proud of.

Finally, to every man reading this who refuses to ride quietly off into the sunset—this is for you. Keep fighting. Keep moving forward. And remember: the storms don't break you. They forge you.

From the bottom of my heart, Thanks!

Dr. Gene Tynes (The Original Antifragile Man)

ABOUT THE AUTHOR

Dr. Gene Tynes is a cowboy at heart, a doctor by training, and a coach by calling. He is also a licensed professional in the Montana Outfitters and Guides Association. With a career spanning decades as a highly respected dentist and a lifetime dedicated to physical, mental, and spiritual transformation, Dr. Tynes has lived the very philosophy he now teaches.

After being forced into early retirement due to health challenges, he didn't slow down — he doubled down on his mission to help men become stronger, wiser, and more grounded with age. Drawing from his own journey from a shy, awkward kid to a confident, capable leader, he created the Genetough method and the Antifragile Man Philosophy — a blueprint for men who want to defy decline and build lasting strength in body, mind, and character.

Today, he works with men around the world to help them rediscover their edge, reclaim their purpose, and model a life of integrity — whether they're just getting started or making the most of their "back nine."

www.ingramcontent.com/pod-product-compliance
Lightning Source LLC
Chambersburg PA
CBHW071731120626
46550CB00002B/482